Knock Down Ginger

Dedication and thanks

For Joan
and her mother
Nellie Lovell

and to thank friends old and new for their contributions without which
Knock Down Ginger would never have come to fruition:

Leslie Barker ('Mr B')
Alf Barrett
Ernie Bright
Audrey Casey
'Bunny' Chambers
John 'JG' Gibson
Ed Gill
Liz Gwyther
A. J. 'Bob' Kimberley
Nellie Armelia Lovell
Chas Mount
Tony Stanley
Johnny Sullivan
Billy Wilkins
Elizabeth Doris Wilkins

and all those named in the text who provided personal recollections .

Ken Kimberley
and friends

Knock Down Ginger

Illustrated tales from younger days

First published in 2004

British Library Cataloguing in
Publication Data
A catalogue record for this book is
available from the British Library.

ISBN 1 85895 222 1

Silver Link Publishing Ltd
The Trundle
Ringstead Road
Great Addington
Kettering
Northants NN14 4BW

Tel/Fax: 01536 330588
email: sales@nostalgiacollection.com
Website: www.nostalgiacollection.com

Printed and bound in Great Britain

The publishing team
at *The* NOSTALGIA *Collection*

Overall management of the project has been in the
hands of **Publisher -** *Peter Townsend,*
who, together with
Freelance Designer - *Karen Stamper,* has been
responsible for the page designs and layouts.

Contents

Introduction

Memories are made of this..

LONDON E13 – 1935

''Ere,' I said to them, as we sat on the railings outside old Dixon's corner shop. 'Alf's getting a football for his birthday.'

With that, and with a wide grin on his face, Alfie came round the corner, and tucked under his arm was a brand new shiny leather football. It was a 'T' ball, the panels shaped into a 'T', just like West Ham played with!

SW PACIFIC – 1945

'This is the Captain speaking. I have received a signal from the Admiral of the Fleet, Admiral Fraser, from GHQ Sydney. It is a signal of historic importance. It reads: "To all ships of the British Pacific Fleet: The Japanese Government, with its military leaders, has accepted the Allies' conditions of Unconditional Surrender. Agreements will be signed on the US Navy Battleship *Missouri* on 2 September in Tokyo Bay, Japan."'

ILFORD, ESSEX – 1948

'Oh, another so-called display man, eh?' he said. 'I wonder how long you'll last?' adding, 'Take this form up to the Labour Exchange and get it signed.

'Crikey,' I wondered, as I hurried along the High Road, 'what 'ave I let myself in for?'

MARBELLA, SPAIN – 1989

It was a hot sticky Saturday afternoon, and I was putting the finishing touches to some fake painted marbling over the high windows that looked out over the swimming pool and beyond. The last bit, thank goodness – I wasn't happy with the scaffolding that had been put up for me. The whole lot gave another wobble. I put one foot on the ladder gathering up my brushes and two pots of paint as I did so. It didn't wobble this time – it swayed far out into the middle of the enormous living-room.

I lay on the white marble floor, the scaffolding, planks and paint covered the marble around me – the white grand piano, which I had insisted be sheeted over, escaped. The phone rang. 'Oh, b***** that,' I thought!

THE BOOK SHOP, UPTON PARK – 1998

The old lady came to the table where I was signing *Oi Jimmy Knacker*.

''Cause,' she said, 'you're not a real cockney, are you? Real East Enders are born the other side of the old iron bridge at Canning Town! Never mind, sign two for me – one's for me brother. He'll like the pictures, luv!'

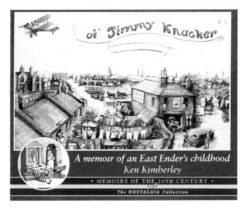

Published in 1998

LAVENHAM – 2000

Roy our postman handed me some letters. 'These two are for you as well, I believe.' I looked at them – the address read 'Author and Artist' Lavenham, Suffolk!

We had a laugh, and he left me on the doorstep, saying, 'The postman always gets his man!'

THE FOLLOWING MONTHS...

My wife Joan would often hand me letters saying, with a cheeky grin on her face, 'More fan mail for you.' They came from around the world and all four corners of the UK.

It seemed that *Jimmy Knacker* had travelled far and wide, and found its way into many hearts, indicating that they, like me, had enjoyed similar experiences in their younger days.

I told Peter Townsend of *Silver Link Publishing* about the letters, and he suggested asking them to enlarge upon their stories. This I did, although in some cases it was like getting blood out of a stone! Nevertheless I persevered and was eventually able to write up and illustrate some happy and some not-so-happy stories!

For me it has been a privilege and a pleasure to do so, and to bring a selection of them all together in *Knock Down Ginger.*

Joan & Ken Kimberley
Spring 2003

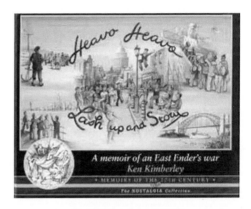

Published in 1999

Balaam Street

Chas Mount

*Sunshine Coast
Eastern Australia*

Balaam Street

In the 1920s, '30s and '40s every town had a Balaam Street. Here you learned the 'three Rs' in your very first school, won a scholarship to higher places or didn't, ran errands to fetch Grandad's Nut Brown from the Red Lion, and carefully carried home Dad's jug of stout or a cupful of mustard pickles for Mum.

If your were lucky enough, every week you got *The Adventure*, *The Wizard* or *The Funny Wonder* – to get all three meant that one day you might become a millionaire!

In the park you could play football (if you could persuade Mrs Chambers to give you back our ball after it had broken her parlour window), play cricket, play hot rice, play marbles or play hooky,

'...carefully carried home Dad's jug of stout...'

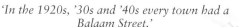

'In the 1920s, '30s and '40s every town had a Balaam Street.'

but you never played on the grass – or played with the girls. You paid 3d for a deckchair, or sat on the railings and listened to the band for nothing.

You could buy lead soldiers, tin soldiers, roller-skates, water pistols, sherbet dabs, bull's-eyes, bubble gum or stick jaw, tennis balls, tops or yo-yos, fishing nets, a pennyworth of broken biscuits, lemonade powder – essentials when you went tiddler-fishing in the long summer holidays, not forgetting one of Mum's old sheets to make a tent in case it rained, which it never did at school holiday time.

'...if you could persuade Mrs Chambers to give you back our ball...'

'...listened to the band...'

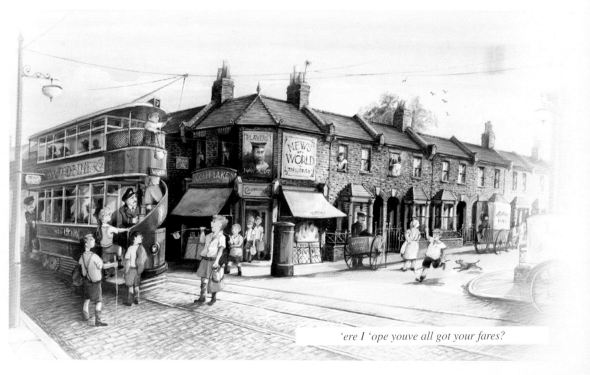

'ere I 'ope youve all got your fares?

Balaam Street never boasted a C&A, *Marks & Spencer* or *Woolworth*s, but the jewel in our crown was *Staddons*, where once a year, like it or lump it, you were 'fitted out', assuming of course that your brother's hand-me-downs didn't fit!

Shoes, socks, shirts and shorts – or, when the time came, your first 'long 'uns' – it was a miserable time, far worse than 'old Cronshaw's' music lesson at school. Then, launched by a stern old lady in black behind a high desk, the hollow wooden ball that contained Dad's hard-earned money whizzed through the air, high above the bargain-hunters below. I watched fascinated!

Balaam Street had five or six pubs that catered for the grown-ups. Folklore has it that deep down in the cellars they were

'Folklore has it that deep down in the cellars they were connected by secret tunnels...'

'...the jewel in our crown was Staddons, where once a year, like it or lump it, you were 'fitted out...'

'It was love at first sight.'

Balaam Street

connected by secret tunnels, enabling unwilling would-be sailors of the 18th century to escape the clutches of the press-gangs that operated in those far-off days on behalf of the Royal Navy.

Down Balaam Street you could go to church – you had to (twice on Sundays) – go to the dentist or doctor, or get a fourpenny 'all off' (haircut), the latter being less popular than the former!

And that's not all… You could also fall in love, because in 'Arry Ponder's greengrocers shop my Dad, on leave from the Western Front in 1916, trod on Mum's foot. It was love at first sight.

Summers and winters came and went – the Roaring Twenties, the anxious Thirties – and 20 years later Balaam Street boys followed in their fathers' footsteps, going their separate ways to France and

Dunkirk, Tobruk or Tunis, to the cold waters of the North Atlantic with the Royal or Merchant Navy or to the airfields of East Anglia, high above the clouds over Hamburg or Berlin or in the jungles of Burma – or to the Salvation Army's hut at Greenock, or – if you were lucky enough – the grandeur of the Stage Door Canteen in New York!

There goes Ernie,
Here comes Alf,
Walking down Balaam Street
Again in our Sunday best.
No MMs to pin on their chests,
No VCs, but we did our best.
We remember those
Who didn't come home;
Rest assured,
You'll never walk alone.

POSTSCRIPT:
Chas Mount, with his wife Sheila, emigrated to Australia in the 1960s, where he joined a company in Melbourne, later becoming Chairman. Chas now lives on Queensland's Sunshine Coast.

The Palace of Varieties

Audrey Casey recalls...

My Dad Gus was born in Tooting, South London, in 1904. He started his working life as a butcher's boy, cycling around the streets of Penge and Sydenham on his butcher's bike, its basket full of choice cuts of meat for the customers of Maloney's Ltd, family butchers of Northwood. A few years later he was promoted and served behind the counter in his smart white apron and boater. Such was his enthusiasm and hard work that he was eventually to become manager.

Maloney's expanded their thriving

'Max Miller, a favourite in those days, was the star turn on the night.'

business and Dad was asked to manage their new shop north of the river in High Street, East Ham E6. The shop was situated between Basses the greengrocers and the London Co-op undertakers; the latter's manager said to Dad so seriously one day, 'Gus, I don't know how you can bear to handle all that cold meat.' Before moving north of the river to East Ham, Mum and Dad married and I came along. Dad earned £5 a week in his manager's job. Mum had come from a well-off family, Dad not so. I realised at an early age that Dad's family were happier with their lot than Mum's family, with all of their extra comforts.

Being a manager Dad was entitled to two weeks' holiday a year. We used to go to Southend – Mum and I went by train, and I used to sit on the suitcases outside the station while she went off to find 'digs'. Later Dad would join us, coming to Southend on his bike to save his fare money. They shopped for food, which the landlady cooked for us. I believe bed and breakfast cost 1 guinea (21 shillings) a week.

Sadly Mum was diagnosed with TB, a dreaded and feared disease of the 1930s, and was sent to a sanatorium at Midhurst in Kent. She was there for many months. Being a manager meant that Dad worked long hours, but instead of leaving me at home when not at school, I would sit in his tiny office at the back of the shop, where I made myself useful doing little odd jobs for him!

Once a month or so Dad would say, 'Come on, our Audrey, we're off to the East Ham Palace of Varieties tonight.' The Palace was just up the High Street, not far from the shop and next door to East Ham station. I would put on my Sunday best and sit beside him, in the front row of the circle, feeling very important and pleased with myself! Not that I could understand much that was going on, but I loved all the colour and the excitement of it, and felt part of it all.

Max Miller, a favourite in those days, was the star turn on the night. As he came on the stage, 'Put your hands over your ears, love,' Dad said. Whatever Dad said I did, not knowing why on this occasion. But I loved Max's bright gaudy clothes, his colourful 'plus-fours' and striped jacket. I turned to Dad, saying, 'Oh look, he's wearing your straw hat.' Everybody was laughing and clapping, so I joined in with them!

Now and again Dad would take me to the dog track at West Ham stadium at Custom House, where he liked to

have a bet on the greyhounds. I cheered with everybody else when the biggest greyhound came in first. 'What are you cheering about, Audrey? I didn't back him! I put my money on the one that came in last.'

Thankfully Mum recovered and came home, but was advised to move to Upminster, considered then to be in the countryside and better for her health. Our mum was never really healthy, but lived on to be 79.

Dad retired, but was never idle even then, tending his lovely garden full of flowers and being very proud of his vegetable patch! Between times came the Second World War, and like thousands of others I wanted to 'do my bit'. I

'What are you cheering about, Audrey?'

joined the ATS, making Dad and Mum very proud of me, telling all the neighbours that their Audrey was in the ATS.

After the war I met and married Dennis, and we had a daughter, Terry. Game to the last, still pottering about in his beloved garden, Dad died in his sleep aged 82. I could go on – there is much more to tell – cos we all know that life is full of ups and downs.

One day perhaps I'll tell the rest of my story!

Personal recollections...

Dear Ken

Many, many thanks for your letter. When reading your book I felt there was so much I could add. Do you remember the Old Lodge in Balaam Street Park opposite the YMCA? It was lived in, with a wrought iron gate on which was a coronet painted in gold. Well, that was the only remaining lodge owned by the Earl of Essex.

Mrs I. Beard

How well I remember playing '*Oi Jimmy Knacker*', marbles, the trips out to the countryside, etc. I was not born till 1940 and lived in Cromwell Road off Green Street, not so far from West Ham football ground, where I was a regular supporter in the 1950s and '60s – the days of John Bond, Noel Cantwell, Ernie Gregory, Ken Brown and many others, not forgetting their great manager, Ted Fenton.

I remember Balaam Street well, and the surrounding areas of Plaistow. My grandfather was an ARP Warden in Rothsay Road and I have a photograph of him and his unit. Trams, trolleybuses – oh, how we miss them! My father used to take me to the docks to see the boats coming in and out, always hoping to get a 'bridger' en route.

Richard Green

What joy it gave me to read your boyhood memories *Oi Jimmy Knacker*. I just had to write to tell you that nearly 20 years later I followed in a lot of your footsteps. Having been brought up in Hollybush Street, I attended Greengate Primary School, referred to by you as Ravenhill Junior Boys' School. Then at 11 I went on to Balaam Street School, by then renamed Burke Secondary Modern. The school your brother attended was by now Plaistow Grammar School. The YMCA building in Greengate Street where you practiced your swimming skills was the building in which I started work in 1959 as an office junior; alas, the swimming pool has gone, and the building now belongs to Green & Silley Weir Shipping Co.

Janice Edwards

The Grand Tour

Eddie Gill   Ernie Bright   Chas Mount   Alf Barrett   Ken Kimberley

Writing to my brother, who was in far-away Canada with the RAF, I told him among other things of my good fortune at Butler & Crispe up at Clerkenwell. I told him how I had been promoted and now had my own ledger, with just two accounts to look after, but big ones: Boots and Timothy Whites & Taylor, the nationally known chemists, and a 3 bob a week rise to go with it. Not bad, eh, Bob, being just 16 years old, adding that I had a week's holiday coming up in June. Me and my old school pals, Chas, Alf, Ernie and Eddy, would probably be out on our bikes every day, to Epping Forest, Lambourne

End, Ongar and all the usual places that we knew so well.

It was early springtime 1942 when Bob wrote back, saying, 'Lucky so-and-sos – wish I was coming with you, though I thought you could be a bit more adventurous. Why don't you join the YHA? Remember when we spent a weekend in Kent?' I certainly did! He and his mate Johnny Sullivan had climbed up the scaffolding to the top of a church tower to take photos of the surrounding countryside. With no head for heights my heart was in my mouth until they got down on to good old 'terra firma'!

During the week I and my mates met, I put the idea to them, and they liked the thought of it. We arranged to have our week's holiday together in June, and they left me to get five YHA membership cards. Luckily for me Ben Tolhurst, who I had sat next to in the counting house, and his wife were keen cyclists in their younger days. Ben told me that the London office was in the Euston Road, opposite Euston Square.

The following lunchtime found me getting off the Inner Circle train at Euston Square, just a few stops from Farringdon Road and close by Clerkenwell Rd. I approached the young lady who sat at the desk.

'I – I mean five of us – want to join the Youth Hostels Association.'

'You are all over 14 years of age?' she asked. I assured her that we were. 'Can I have your names and addresses?' she asked, and after signing this and that and handing her the necessary 5 bob (1 shilling) each, we all became paid-up members of the YHA.

As I handed the cards around I explained that it cost 3 shillings a night, wherever we stayed. This included a hot meal on arrival, breakfast and, if we wanted it, a packet of sandwiches to take with us the next morning, but these would cost extra. I also explained that the warden at each hostel could ask us to do some small jobs around the place, such as helping with the washing up, sweeping the paths, or washing down the tables where we had our food. Enthusiastic now, where we should go was the big question. Looking back now to all those years ago, our choice was a bit foolhardy, as we chose the West Country, which meant cycling through parts of bomb-scarred London and beyond.

All working in the City, or thereabouts, we boasted that we knew our way about. It would mean biking from the east side to the far west side, with little knowledge of the streets in those parts, having never been west of Oxford Street in our young lives! Of course, we dismissed this in our enthusiasm. I phoned the YHA office to reserve the accommodation on the route we had planned, after poring over a well-worn map. Winchester would be our first port of call, about 70 miles distant, Sutton Veney, not far from Winchester, for the second and third nights, Batheaston next, on to Marlborough and then Reading, or thereabouts, for our last night. This proved a problem because Reading was fully booked, so it meant staying two nights in Marlborough. 'Oh, that's OK,' we all agreed. Everything now settled, we eagerly waited for our holiday to come round.

The long-awaited Sunday morning in June came at last and at 7.30am, in the early morning sunshine, I met Eddy outside Romford Station. We went down Crow Lane, past the cemetery and Romford Gas Works, and eventually knocked on Alf's door in Becontree half an hour later. Alf was waiting for us and raring to go! Mr and Mrs Barrett waved to us. 'Look after yourselves!' his Mum called out, then we were off to Plaistow E13 to pick up Ernie and Chas, who were both waiting for us outside the Greengate Pub. We had all been bombed out during the Blitz days, Alf, Eddy and me moving to the Essex outskirts, Ernie and Chas moving not far from their original homes.

It was a happy band that

'...to pick up Ernie and Chas, who were both waiting for us outside the Greengate Pub.'

waited for the traffic lights to change at Gardiner's Corner, Aldgate, then it was on through the bomb-scarred city, past St Paul's, with its huge dome still there, its cross glistening as ever above the burnt-out remains of the surrounding buildings, up through High Holborn, Shaftsbury Avenue, Leicester Square and along the Embankment close by the River Thames. Of course all the signposts had been removed while the threat of invasion lingered. On our own territory this was no problem, but by which bridge to cross the river was a problem, and our first big headache. After an hour Charlie said, 'Look Ken, I'm sure we've crossed the river two or three times on different bridges!' Out came the tattered old map, which proved of little use.

'Oh, I'll ask this old lad.' I explained that we were looking for the right road to take us to Winchester. He looked us over, with the signs of frustration and weariness already settling over us. 'Crikey, lads!

You've a fair way to go – you're in Kingston-upon-Thames, or nearby,' he said. 'You want Guildford. Keep on this road and you'll be all right. You've to get up the Hog's Back. You'll find you have to walk up there – not many get up the "Back" on their bikes, I can tell you! That'll take you down to Farnham, from there you'll pick up the A31, and that'll take you right down. The 31 is a busy road, even on Sundays, so mind how you go, boys,' he said, taking a big watch from his waistcoat pocket. 'Hmm, it's about one now, with a bit of luck you should be in Winchester by six. Good luck, lads.'

Knowing now that we were pointing in the right direction, all the early morning enthusiasm returned and it was just after 6 when we spotted the old water mill boasting its YHA sign, just before Winchester Cathedral, with its towering spire, came into view. As we signed the register we were pleased with ourselves, Chas saying knowingly that we had biked through three counties – Essex, Surrey and now Hampshire. We had come about 80 miles too!

We sat down to our supper. It was a tasty hot meal that we all scoffed up, chattering to the other occupants, mostly young like ourselves. 'You come from London?' they asked. 'What's it like up there? Is it true what the papers say?'

'Something like,' we answered. 'Not so bad now, though.' They were from the Midlands and Wales and hadn't copped it so badly as we had up in 'the Smoke'. We paid 3 shillings for our night's stay and ninepence for our packet of sandwiches.

It was a cloudy, overcast morning with rain threatening as we set off for Sutton Veney, and after 5 miles or so down it came. We stopped and got into our waterproof capes. 'Crikey!' said Eddy as

'...with a bit of luck you should be in Winchester by six.' the old lad said.

he got under his, 'it's full of holes! I took it off me Dad's bike thinking it would be all right.' Thankfully the rain eased off.

As I had organised the trip I was looked upon as a navigator of sorts! With no signposts and a weather-worn old map, it was proving difficult, never more so that when, 15 miles or so from Winchester, at the bottom of a hill, I was horrified to brake in front of a large sign in the middle of the road, surrounded by coils of ugly-looking barbed wire stretching off left and right. To the right was a concrete bunker like those we had seen many times in our travels around Essex when the German invasion had seemed imminent. To add to my concern, beyond the barbed wire was a sandy beach and the grey-looking sea! 'Oh crikey!' I thought, 'a bloomin' fine navigator I've turned out to be!'

I must have taken the wrong road out of Winchester and led us all 15 miles or so out of our way!' I thought of Bob's words, about being a bit more adventurous. At that moment I wished we'd stuck to dear old Essex!

'What do we do now, Ken?' Alf asked.

'I dunno, Alf – looks as if I've made a right balls-up!' I replied with more than a hint of frustration in my voice, but they all took it in good part, and an hour or so later we found the right road to Sutton Veney. An hour later, without knowing it, we crossed the Hampshire boarder into Wiltshire and the rain came down again, with a strong wind. Poor Eddy, his holed cape soon became worse as the wind finally reduced it to streamers that flew behind him like old flags! We stopped and in turn offered the loan of ours – after all, he was just 14, and in a way we felt responsible for him. He took what was left of it off and dumped it in a nearby ditch, then I went off in front with Ernie, Eddy followed close behind, and Alf and Chas brought up the rear, hoping it would afford

'...as the wind finally reduced it to streamers that flew behind him like old flags!'

'...beyond the barbed wire was a sandy beach and the grey-looking sea!'

Eddy some protection from the weather. Capes or not, we were all soaked when we finally arrived at the hostel in Sutton Veney.

'Crikey lads! You've had a rough day of it!' the warden said when we five stood in front of him and signed in. 'Look, get into the dormitory, get into a change of clothes and my wife will dry them out for you over the kitchen boiler.' We thankfully did as he suggested and a tired but still enthusiastic bunch sat down to a well-earned and welcome hot supper. That brought day two of our grand tour to a close! Before turning in I looked at the *Guide to Winchester* that I had picked up off the warden's desk. I passed it to Ernie, who seemed his usual chirpy exuberant self after our long and very wet, windy day. He opened it with interest. ''Ere, did you know that Winchester is the county town of Hampshire and is 66 miles from London?' Our legs had told us that the day before! 'In the old castle is the so-called table of King Arthur, where he wined and dined his knights and noblemen. Near the city is the Hospital of St Cross, founded in 1136 for poor old men.'

'Like us!' we chorused together.

'Cor, listen to this,' Ernie went on. 'Winchester was founded in Roman times and was the capital of Wessex. For 200 years before the Norman Conquest it was the capital of England! What do you think about that, then?'

Next morning, Tuesday, the kind warden's wife placed at the end of the table our clothes from the day before, ironed and neatly folded! We thanked her, paid for our board, collected our packed lunches and popped a few coppers into the local church's collection box. 'Is there anything we can do for you before we leave?' we asked the warden's wife.

'That's all right boys – hope you have a nicer day!' It was a real scorcher as we set off for Batheaston, thankfully not too far away, just 30 miles. 'Piece of cake!' we all thought. Batheaston was a short distance from the city of Bath. We arrived early and found the hostel as welcoming as the others. Before our meal we had a short stroll around the village, admiring the thatched cottages, although Alf didn't, remembering his evacuation days spent in one!

'We found our way into the famous baths...'

We sat down outside the local pub and, feeling pleased with ourselves, we ventured inside. 'I'm 'aving a cider,' Chas said, and we all followed suit. 'Rough or smooth?' we were asked. Not knowing the difference and not wishing to show our ignorance in grown-up matters, we all asked for rough. Fifteen minutes later we left our rough cider on the table outside. 'We'll know better next time!' Chas said.

The next day we cycled into the ancient spa city and strolled around, admiring the clean, well-kept shops and houses, untouched by the war, so it seemed. We found our way into the famous baths and, with a guide's help, admired the colonnades and its carved stonework. He pointed out the mosaic floors that we had only ever seen in our history books down at Balaam Street School, but here it was all real, in front of our very eyes. In Roman days it had been called 'Aquae Sulis' and the guide proudly told us that the city's Roman remains were the best in Great Britain!

We decided on another visit the next day, but freewheeling down the long hill just outside the city two smashing-looking girls, going in the opposite direction, waved to us. Minutes later Eddy called out, 'I can't see Ernie! Something's happened to 'im.' We stopped – surely he hadn't left us and gone chasing after those two girls, we asked each other. Our Ernie wasn't like that, we thought! Charlie, thinking he was maybe missing out on things, said, 'We'd better go back and look for him.' We turned round and pushed our bikes up the long incline. The last thing on Ernie's mind when we eventually found him by his upturned bike on the grass verge was the two girls. Chas, I thought, looked a little disappointed! Of course Ernie knew that we would go back for him, and we kept our thoughts to ourselves as we helped mend the puncture, but to no avail, for the inner tube was beyond repair.

An hour later our bikes were leaning against the railings of Bath Abbey, with Ernie's upturned bike a bit of an embarrassment as passers-by glanced at us and hurried past. 'Anybody would think we were begging!' remarked Charlie. 'Bit of a snooty lot around 'ere, if you ask me!' he declared.

'Cor, it made an 'ole in me pocket – 1s 11d it cost me!' said Ernie on his return with a brand new inner tube over his shoulder. With the new tube and tyre at last back in place, the question now was what to do with the old tube! 'Got no room for it in my saddlebag.' We all said the same. Cheeky Eddy, being the bravest of us, said, 'Oh, give it 'ere!' and draped it over the ornate railings.

'You can't leave it there, Eddy!'

'Oh can't I? Just watch me!' as he pedalled off. The rest of us quickly followed suit and scarpered off out of Bath as fast as we could!

We spent the rest of the day, not as we had intended, but pedalling up hill and thankfully freewheeling down the other side on this glorious summer's day, the breathtaking views of the Somerset countryside living with us for the rest of our days! We stopped for our packed lunch and downed a pint of sweet cider this time! We passed the warden's office on our return and heard the crackling wireless giving out the sombre news that General Rommel had, with his Afrika Corps, surrounded the Western Desert outpost of Tobruk in North Africa. The announcer went on to say that Malta was under siege and that higher losses were being incurred in the desperate Battle of the Atlantic. Young as we were, we were in no two minds about the final outcome: we sang, 'Our boys will hang out their washing on the Siegfried Line.'

We spent our last night in Batheaston. 'See you next summer!' the cheerful

warden said. 'Sure thing!' we replied,
little realising then that our thoughts
12 months hence would not be of
another 'Grand Tour' but of
which of the armed
forces –
Navy,

*'...we eventually found him
by his upturned bike on the
grass verge...'*

told us as we wheeled our
bikes out in the early morning
sunshine.

'Crikey!' exclaimed Chas, 'that
means 100 miles for us!'

Thankfully the hot weather had given
way to cooler conditions and thankfully
it also remained dry. With heads down
the miles slipped away as lots of Army
convoys went past us heading west.

'They're Yanks,' Chas called out.
Their uniforms were unfamiliar
to us, but they all gave us a
friendly wave.

Army or Air Force – we would be joining!
We headed back east to Mar!borough
where we intended to stay for our last
two nights. We left Somerset behind us
and were once again back in Wiltshire,
the countryside proving as delightful
as that in Somerset. We explored the
Marlborough Downs where flocks of
sheep grazed, without a care in
the world! The second day
found us high up on the
Hampshire Downs, all
strenuous biking, but us
never-say-die kids were up
to it and forgot the war,
although we probably had
more stops now than at the
week's beginning.

'How far is it to
London?' we asked
the warden on our last
morning.

'A good 80 miles,' he

*'...and draped it over the
ornate railings.'*

A jeep waved us down. 'Hey, you guys!' It was the first Yankee jeep that we had ever set eyes on, except at the pictures! 'Hold your horses, men, there's some really wide trucks coming through in a few minutes.'

There was, too – they were huge transporters with tanks on board. A driver leaned from the high-up cab. 'Thanks, guys!' he said as he waved us on our way. Our stops became more frequent, but with heads down we kept at it!

The clock on the front of the department store at Gardiner's Corner, Aldgate, said 6.10pm, and here, of all places, old Ernie got his second puncture of the week, the front wheel this time. Luckily for us it was the weekend – a weekday would have found us in the busiest spot in East London. We leaned our bikes against the windows of this famous old East End store; everybody knew Gardiner's Corner, E1. We helped him fix the puncture, but weariness had set in now, as Ed mumbled, 'Dunno about new tyres, Ern, you want to treat yourself to a new bike!'

Our weary legs took us up the Commercial Road with its cobblestones shaking the life out of our bikes, being careful to avoid the dreaded tramlines that at times drew you to them like a magnet. The emptiness and scarred remains of bombed-out streets brought us finally back to earth with a mighty bump!

We went past Burdett Road, Limehouse, where my old Gran was born, and Poplar High Street, where Mum went to school and Alf's parents were born, over the Canning Town Bridge and along the Barking Road to the Greengate public house, the

'The clock on the front of the department
store at Gardiner's Corner, Aldgate, said
6.10pm...'

surrounding streets having been our playground of just a few years before. We left Chas at our schoolboy haunts and went on to the Boleyn Pub at Upton Park, close by West Ham FC's ground.

'See you on Monday!' I said to Ernie, as we worked together in the same office up at Clerkenwell.

We sat outside Alf's place 45 minutes later. 'Come in for a drink?' he asked us.

'No thanks,' Eddy answered for the both of us. 'If I get off me bike, I'll never get back on again!'

It was just a week ago that we had all set off on our Grand Tour, I thought. I left Eddy outside Romford Station. 'You'll be all right?' I asked him.

'Whatcha mean? 'Course I will.' He gave me a wave and set off for North Romford. I pedalled up the hill in Victoria Road, Romford, and at long last turned into Brooklands Gardens.

Paddy gave me his familiar bark as I knocked at the door. 'Have a nice week?'

Mum asked, adding, 'You look worn out! I'll put the kettle on and make you a nice cup of tea.' Paddy came bounding in from the passage with his tennis ball between his teeth, jumping up on my lap as if to say, 'When are we going out then?'

'Oh, give us a break old son!' I said as I drank the best cup of tea I had had for a week!

I wondered if they all felt as I did, worn out but a bit pleased, and a little proud of ourselves!

'I'll write to Bob next week and tell him how we got on!'

"Ere, Ken,' Ernie said to me in the office on Monday morning. With his head for figures, he reckoned we had biked nearly 400 miles! All for 35 bob, although he added that it cost an extra 1s 11d for the new inner tube!

Bombers passing overhead reminded us of nights spent in the Anderson shelter.

Personal recollections...

My mum and dad were horrified when I told them of my wish to go on the 'Grand Tour' with my mates, "Don't you realise there is war on" they said- perhaps you may never get home!
Thankfully my Gran intervened saying "Oh let him go, it will be an experience for him to get away from all of these bomb sites and ruins, and out into the countryside with all his mates".
We did that alright 400 miles of it- it was a good effort from a bunch of kids- or should I say saddle sore kids!

Chas Mount

My brother Jack would begrudgingly loan me his bike - only on dull days - but never when it was raining or threatened to do so.
However I did persuade him to loan it to me to go on the 'Grand Tour' with the other lads-on condition that I never got it wet!
We encountered a few fine days on our travels but many wet and muddy ones.
Thankfully for me, arriving back, Jack wasn't home, so I was able to wash 400 miles of rain and mud of his beloved bike, and was able to return it to him in its usual pristine condition!
I darn't tell him though, that I had had two punctures.

Ernie Bright

It was our first holiday experience after leaving school where we had been close friends. Away from bomb scarred London was like a return to normality, and I fondly recall the humour that kept us going when facing wind and rain- sixty years on we still recall the cycling holiday when we meet.

Alf Barrett

At times I blessed and cursed my brother for suggesting that we should be a little more adventurous on our weeks holiday.
At times I wished we had stuck to our well known haunts like Epping Forest and good old Lambourne End and the like.
For some reason not known to this day I was appointed the 'Navigator'.
After loosing our way for the umpteenth time.
Chas Mount turned to me saying "Ken never join the Navy-cos I'm certain you'll lead the fleet up Barking Creek"
Apart from all that , it was 7 days that I will forever remember.

Ken Kimberley

Remembering the 1930s and 1940s

'Bunny' Chambers

The school bell stopped ringing. 'They'll be coming up soon,' I said to myself. I could hear the tramp, tramp of boots and shoes as the classes filed up the stone staircase at Balaam Street School, E13.

'No skylarking about there!' I could hear above the noise, as I and the other monitors endeavoured to keep order on the staircase.

This was to be my last term at school, then it was to be out in the wide, wide world. Doing what, I wondered? Forty or so other lads had the same thought on their minds I suppose, though I had another six months or so to think about it all. I knocked at the classroom door of 4A, then we opened the door and hurried in. Old Cohn peered at us over his horn-rimmed specs and waved us to our places. 'No bad boys today?' he asked. We all chorused, 'No, Sir.'

Peggy, Jean and Louise sat around the table. Mum placed a plate of bread slices in front of us, together with our favourite jar of jam. It was too early for Dad and Wally, my older brother, to be home from work. Mum poured us out a cup of tea. Finishing my tea, I walked up the passage and left them to listen to *Children's Hour* on our wireless, with its accumulator and battery alongside it.

'Bernie,' Mum called, 'your Dad wants you to get the accumulator changed Saturday morning, so don't forget to, will you?'

'...the tramp, tramp of boots and shoes as the classes filed up the stone staircase...'

'Of course not, Mum,' I replied. I went out into the now dark winter street, and joined Ken, 'Spud' Taylor and Eddy, who as usual were sitting on the railings outside old Dixon's corner shop.

'What we doing tonight?' I asked. 'We owe old Ma one,' 'Spud' said. 'Remember when she kept our ball when it went through her parlour window? We said sorry. Made no different though. After all, it wasn't our fault – remember, it hit the curb and bounced up over her railings.'

'Trouble was, it knocked her aspidistra off its stand,' I said.

'Spud' produced a reel of black thread. 'This'll do nicely,' he said, and we all agreed; 'Spud' knew all about such things. 'Bernie,' he said to me, 'tie this end to her knocker – don't make any noise.' A dim light, coming through the fanlight, lit up the door knocker. 'Not so much noise,' he whispered. By now Alf, Eddy and Kenny had shinned up the sewer wall; this was easy, but the Carpenters had painted it with a red, white and blue distemper for the Jubilee, and it was beginning to wear off, specially when you climbed up it – you got smothered!

I gave the reel to 'Spud', who hurried across the road and passed it up to Ken's outstretched hand. 'Spud' bunked me up

'Trouble was, it knocked her aspidistra off its stand.'

the wall, and he followed. We heard old man Hennesy's dog bark in the corner house at the end of the sewer wall. It was a ferocious-looking alsatian, and we all gave it a wide berth when we set eyes on it! We must have disturbed it, I thought. All now gathered with heads just peeking over the top of the wall. 'Not yet,' 'Spud' called to me. 'There's somebody coming.'

'Crikey, Kenny,' I said, 'it's your Mum. She's just coming home from work.' A few others who had got off the tram and buses up at the top followed her.

In a minute the street became deserted again. 'Spud' whispered, 'Now, Bernie.' I obliged, and the faint tap-tap of the knocker could be heard as I gently pulled the cotton reel. The passage light went on and old Ma peered left and right to see who had disturbed her evening.

'Not yet, Bunny. Let her get sat down again.'

However, I didn't have a chance to let old Ma get settled down again because with leaps, bounds and growls, old Hennesy's alsatian came leaping towards us. 'Oh crikey!' said 'Spud' as a he heaved himself up over the sewer wall and fell into the street below. I followed suit, and Kenny chased off towards the Carpenters' house; in doing so he let out a yell, as his foot caught a discarded iron barrel ring, which must have given him a real smacker on the knee.

Alf ran off in the direction from which

the alsatian had come. The dog skidded to a halt and went hell for leather after him; Kenny said later that he had never seen Alf run so fast. Nevertheless, as Alf came to his backyard fence, which faced Dongola Road, the dog caught up and nipped his trousers. The big teeth drew blood, but his biggest worry was what was he going to tell his Mum!

Eddy watched all the fun from the shadows cast by the street lamp, not daring to go home with his suit covered in red, white and blue distemper! 'Spud' was worrying that his Mum would miss her reel of thread – we had left it on the sewer bank.

'...tie this end to her knocker – don't make any noise...'

Coming from the city, some No 23 buses would turn round in Holly Bush Street, at the back of the Greengate public house, the conductor and driver taking their tea-break at the same time. The conductor would take the opportunity to empty the box of used tickets into the kerbside – they were all colours and as stiff as cardboard, and us kids could make all sorts of things with them, specially in the dark winter evenings. With some of Mum's flour and water we could make a rich creamy paste and, hey presto, we could make wind wheels; the tickets were pasted together and cut into a circle with the centres cut out triangle-fashion. Taken out into the

street, specially Dongola Road, on a windy day, we would chase after them – oh, the fun we had with those used tickets!

As I picked up the nearest and cleanest ones and stuffed them into my pockets, I couldn't believe my eyes, for lying among them was an almost brand new one-pound note! Together with the tickets I stuffed it in my pocket and hurried off to school.

'Wake up, Chambers!' old Cohn called. 'What are you dreaming of?' I didn't tell him. I was busy thinking what I was to do with my pound note. At 4 o'clock, instead of going home, I ran through all the back alleyways to Queen Road market, and headed for the stall that sold chocolate bars and every other sweet you could think of. I had made up my mind. 'Six bars of these,' I said to the fat lady in the white apron. 'Cadbury's fruit and nut.'

'Can you afford them?' she asked me with a suspicious look on her face. I hastily thrust the pound note into her open hand. She put the sweets in a paper bag and gave me a lot of change!

I had always wanted a torch, all glistening and silver-looking, just like the ones they had in the pictures, though not as big, of course. I ran to the stall that sold them. I pointed to the one I wanted. 'Batteries are extra,' he said.

My pockets were bulging with all my goodies, so before Mum opened the door I whipped my coat off. 'You're late home,' she said.

'I've been in the park looking for caterpillars.'

Up in bed that night I handed a *Cadbury's* fruit and nut bar to each of my brothers and sisters. 'Don't tell Mum and Dad I've given these to you, promise?' I asked each one in turn. We had a midnight feast! I tucked my torch safely under my pillow. The excitement of it all kept me awake, and in the early hours I shone my torch through the window and spied old man Ebbage's cat sitting on our fence.

Sitting down at my desk the next morning, I put my 'find' on the top of the desk between the inkwells, making sure

that everybody could see it – old Cohn couldn't because we all knew he was short-sighted! This was a big mistake – everybody admired my torch. 'Where did you find it, Bunny?' they all asked me.

'I didn't – I bought it.'

'Fibber!' they all said. To make matters worse, back at home Mum found chocolate wrappers upstairs under the blankets. That was the start of the big interrogation. Where, where, how, how, Mum and Dad demanded to know.

'Take them out to the back,' Dad said to Mum. 'I'm going to get to the bottom of this.' To me he said, 'Sit down there.' Dad sat opposite me at the kitchen table. 'I want the truth, Bernie – where did you get the money from?' adding, 'The truth, Bernie.'

I explained how I found the pound note. 'Is that the truth, Bernie, cos even if you're my son I won't have a thief living under my roof.'

'Course it is, Dad, course it is. Honest! Honest it is!'

Dad came round the table, put his hand on my shoulder and said, 'I believe you, son – go and tell the others they can come in.'

Before going to school the next morning Mum handed me a sealed envelope addressed to Mr Cohn. 'Your father wants you to give this to Mr Cohn.' I did so. At 4 o'clock, before leaving the classroom, Mr Cohn handed me a letter. 'Give this to your father, Chambers.' I did so, and not another word was ever said about my find again.

Six months later I made my way to Snowhill Labour Exchange in the heart of the City and was lucky

'The conductor would take the opportunity to empty the box of used tickets into the kerbside...'

straight away. I was sent to the Parker Pen Company in Bush House in the Strand. I produced my report at the interview. 'Jolly good, young man, jolly good. Report to the service department next Monday at 8.30am.'

It was 1936 and my wage was 12s 6d a week. On the way home to Plaistow on the District Line, I thought, 'No more cleaning the knives and forks, spoons and what have you, Dad's boots – after all, I am a wage-earner now.' Mum quickly put me right on this. As ever, newspapers were spread out over the kitchen table, out came the metal polish, and I still had to get cleaning and polishing with the rest of 'em. All the bits were lined up for Dad's inspection. 'That fork could do with a bit more elbow grease,' he would say. At last he would be satisfied, and the cutlery was carefully returned to the dresser drawer!

Together with my former schoolmates I acquired a bike (second-hand), and often on Saturday afternoons we would meet and head off for Epping, Bishop's Stortford and eventually Saffron Walden, where we would spend the night under the stars, in the shelter of a haystack.

Those happy carefree days came to an end in September 1939. I was 16, still working in London, and quickly became aware of all the young men in their smart uniforms with polished buttons, polished boots, be they Navy, Army or Air Force – especially as, more often than not, they had a girl on their arm!

The Parker Pen Company quickly lost its appeal, although I was doing all right. Sitting on the train to E13, I gloomily thought it would be another 12 months or more before I could get into a uniform! And get a girl. Then I had a great idea. 'I'll tell them I'm 18 at the recruiting centre,' I said to Lou.

'D'yer think I look 18, Lou?'

'No,' he said, 'you look 58, Bernie.' I took a swipe at him, and Lou with his cricket ball went off to Balaam Street park to get a game of cricket. He was a demon bowler, and never had a job getting a game, providing he was on your side – not so much with the bat, but with the ball he was a terror!

Dunkirk came and went, and soon afterwards the bombs rained down on the East End, and with hundreds of others we lost our home and everything in it. We were re-housed in Flanders Road, East Ham, just up the Barking Road. From that day I lost touch with all of my mates in Plaistow – like us they were scattered far and wide!

Shortly after, bold as brass, I went into the nearest Army recruiting office and gave my age as 18, when really I was just

'Dad sat opposite me at the kitchen table. "I want the truth, Bernie…"'

17 years old, or nearly. Mum and Dad were furious when I eventually let on.

A few months later I walked up Warley Hill in Brentwood, Essex, home of the Essex Regiment, where I commenced three months' infantry training. It was May 1941. Did I get a girl when I at last got into uniform? I can't remember! Since Warley Barracks was just 12 miles from home in East Ham, I managed to enjoy some of Mum's home cooking every other weekend when not on guard duty, returning back to barracks late on Sunday evening with my pal Joe Wilkinson – we called him 'Bluey' after the famous West Ham speedway star 'Bluey Wilkinson.'

All good things come to an end, and I got a posting to Hampshire, where I stayed for three weeks. I then had a shock for I got an overseas posting, and had to report to the Quartermaster's store to collect my foreign service kit, with helmet and all the rest of it! With it went seven days' embarkation leave. There were a lot of tears shed around the house when I said goodbye to them all, as in so many homes in those long-ago days.

I boarded the train at Euston with lots of other lads, then waiting for us at the quayside was the former passenger liner *Ormondie*. Of course the big question was where we were going. One wag suggested, 'Iceland.' We badgered the crew to tell us, but being wise old hands they wouldn't let on, only to say that it was the biggest convoy the *Ormondie* had sailed in!

After nearly three weeks at sea, often witnessing far-off destroyer escorts dropping depth-charges, we arrived in Valletta Harbour, Malta. There we were transferred from the Essex Regiment to the 1st Battalion of the Hampshires, to bring the latter up to full strength, not knowing that an operation was being planned for the invasion of North Africa.

On 7 November 1942 we boarded another 'trooper' with supply ships of all shapes and sizes, and landing crafts heavily escorted by the Royal

'...more often than not, they had a girl on their arm!'

Navy. Off the North African coast we went over the side, down the scramble nets, into the LCIs below. Anybody who thinks that the Med is always blue and calm can think again, what with the heaving and tossing about, then getting closer inshore the shelling started from Jerry's 88mm guns.

Then came the Stukas with a terrifying shriek as they came down vertically at us. I closed my eyes, as I'm sure most of the lads did. I remember seeing Dad and hearing him saying 'Now tell me the truth, Bernie' as if it was a dream. I heard the bottom of the LCI hit the beach, the rattle as the front dropped, then, 'Off we go, lads,' I heard as I opened my eyes. 'Come on, Bunny, you've got to get ashore.'

I made it, but some of my mates weren't so lucky. We fought our way up to Tunis, where the campaign in North

'Dunkirk came and went, and soon afterwards the bombs rained down on the East End…'

Africa came to an end on 12 May 1943, but there was still a long, long way to go, heart-breaking at times for so many, but historians have told us since that it was the beginning of the end for the German and Italian forces. The Regiment was taken out of the line and along the North African coast to Sfax, where we rested for a month, to be told that preparations were being made for the invasion of Sicily. We joined the 40th Marine Commandos and landed with them at Cape Pachino on 10 July 1943. We went ashore with the independent Malta Brigade and the 1st Dorsets and 2nd Devonshires.

As ever Jerry put up a strong resistance, but we fought our way up to Ragusfa, across the Catonia Plains and at last Messina, and the Germans evacuated Sicily on 17 August 1943 for the Italian mainland.

During a respite, we became anxious at not having heard from home for months. We were all in the same boat, which eased our individual fears, especially as we became aware that the German bombing of the UK had eased considerably – indeed, the boot was now on the

'Off the North African coast we went over the side, down the scramble nets...'

'He climbed the small dais. "I am here to tell you..."'

other foot. Jerry was getting a taste of what he had dished out to us during the early 1940s. Of course this boosted our spirits, for what we knew lay ahead of us.

The buzz went around that we could expect a visit from a VIP. It was the big chief himself, General Montgomery of the 8th Army – he was instantly recognisable with that famous beret, hawk-like nose, and upright figure, as stiff as a board.

He climbed the small dais. 'I am here to tell you...' 'That we're all going home,' a voice from the back called out.

He cupped a hand to his ear. 'What was that I heard? Speak up, man, I didn't hear you.'

The cheeky, very brave voice repeated itself. The General heard the voice this time round. 'Not just yet, my man – we all have a little job to do across the Straits before they let you and I get back to blighty.'

'...all surprise was lost, and we got more than a warm welcome...'

There was much laughter at this, and from then on he became one of us! He became our 'Monty'. He went on, 'You men will be the first to set foot on mainland Europe since Dunkirk, and you will not have long to wait!'

'When can we expect to get some letters from home, Monty?' another brave voice called out.

'I'll look into it,' he promised, 'and another thing, as I don't smoke, drink,' adding, 'nor swear, I've saved my rations to give to you lot. That is all, except to wish you good luck and God be with you all.' With that he was gone.

We checked our rations – bully beef, tin of stew, two boiled sweets, dry milk, tea and sugar, a small Tommy cooker heated by camphor blocks, and the extra fags as promised by 'Monty' – enough to last two men two days!

The weather turned rough as we headed across the Straits of Messina. Our ETA was 5.30am, destination the beaches of Reggio di Calabris. Owing to worsening weather we arrived 2 hours late, all surprise was lost, and we got more than a warm welcome.

We reached the main coast road. I was attached to 'A' Company as support Vickers machine-gunner, and was soon confronted by German troop-carriers towing 88mm guns, well supplied with ammunition trucks and the rest of it.

The Company spread out into the surrounding heavy undergrowth, and succeeded in knocking out the 88s with their crews. We laid low, waiting for our own reinforcements to arrive from the beach head, but the Germans re-grouped.

'On the third day he came running excitedly back into the cave: "British Tommies are here!"'

Down the road from our positions we could see Panzer tanks, supported by Stukas, with their troop-carriers bringing up the rear. Our position became hopeless – we returned as much fire as we could, but the order came down the line: scatter and be prepared to be taken prisoner.

I partly dismantled my Vickers and tossed it into the surrounding vine groves, Jerry bullets whizzing all about me. My luck finally ran out – it had to happen. I felt this searing red hot pain in my right arm, just below my shoulder. I staggered on, came to the edge of the vine grove, and faced an outcrop of rocks and boulders. Staggering about now, I came to a small opening and squeezed inside, realising that I must now be behind German lines.

In the darkness three or four faces stared at me, and I stared back, now with my left hand clenched over my wound.

My luck was in again – they were a young Italian family taking shelter. Today I thank God that they were friendly towards me. The father took off his shirt, ripped it into pieces and bandaged my arm and shoulder as best he could. For two days they gave me food and drink, while their son informed me of the German troop movements.

On the third day he came running excitedly back into the cave: 'British Tommies are here!' He was right – our reinforcements had pushed Jerry back. He came back with a stretcher-bearer party. I thanked them from the bottom of my heart, and came round at a beach dressing station, where I was patched up and put on a landing craft that took me back

'I struggled up and looked below.'

to Catavina in Sicily. My fighting days were over! It was 10 September 1943.

I was patched up, put on a Red Cross Dakota with other wounded, and flown to Egypt. I vaguely remember the pilot calling out, 'Those who can, look below.' I struggled up and looked below. There, 'in line astern' as the pilot said, was the remnants of the Italian fleet. Leading the line was a heavy RN cruiser, with 12 or so destroyers streaming out port and starboard in close attendance. They were on their way to Valletta in Malta to surrender to the Royal Navy.

An hour or so later we landed and were transferred to a New Zealand field hospital, where I had a preliminary operation. Days later I was put on the hospital ship *Ascania* and taken to the Nile delta, where I spent the next 12 months transferring from one British Army hospital to another. Unbeknown to me, being constantly on the move meant that my mail never caught up with me. My eldest brother Wally was stationed with the Essex Regiment on the Isle of Wight, and to date that had been the extent of his 'foreign service'. I discovered this when out of the blue one letter eventually

turned up for me. I didn't recognise the handwriting as it was from a Miss Maureen Wightman; Wally had befriended her family, and was often invited to tea on a Sunday.

At last my family had received a telegram from the Infantry Record Office at Warwick telling them of my wounds. Wally, telling his friends of my plight, asked Mrs Wightman's daughter Maureen if she would write to me in an effort to cheer me up, as it had been two years since I had last heard from home! She eventually did with an 'air-graph letter', which arrived just after Christmas Day 1943. I was in the 16th General Hospital at the time, and what a late Christmas present it was! So too were all the letters from home that finally caught up with me.

After yet another move to the 23rd General, nine months later I was finally discharged, unfit for active duties. It was now September 1944, and I was sent to convalesce under canvas for three

months at El Ballah. Maureen and I continued to write to each other. At the end of three months I was assessed and the doctor confirmed that my infantry days were over. I went to Ismailia with little to do, then on to GHQ at Cairo to join the Royal Army Service Corps (RASC), and eventually joined the 591 Car Company, which proved to be a car pool for officers working in GHQ. I explained to the Sergeant, 'Look, I can't drive.'

'No worries about that, lad – get in the jeep and I guarantee you'll be driving around Cairo in a week.' I was too, much to my amazement! After a month or so I was astonished to find myself chauffeuring the Chief of Imperial Staff, General Oliver, and his aide. For this job I was made up to Corporal, as the stripes went with the job!

It was a flag car, a pre-war Humber Pullman, and we were escorted by Army Red Corps in a jeep. Often I would drive him to an RAF airstrip near Cairo, where

'...I was astonished to find myself chauffeuring the Chief of Imperial Staff...'

he would be flown back to the UK; while there he would inform my mother, in some way or another, how her Bernard was doing. I was so grateful to him for doing this, that when he asked me to serve in Cairo for a further six months, I found it difficult to refuse him!

I was his driver for two years or more, and Maureen and I continued to exchange letters, every one becoming more precious to me than the last. Part of the 'deal' I had with the General was that he would arrange four weeks' leave for me. He must have pulled a few strings, because I left Port Suez on the destroyer *Battle Axe* and was put ashore at Toulon on the French coast near Marseilles. Days later I arrived at Dieppe and boarded the *Isle of Thanet*, which took me to Newhaven. I put my foot on English soil for the first time in six years, and was now 24.

It was a wonderful moment for me, one that I shall never forget, when I saw Wally, my eldest brother, beyond the barrier at Waterloo Station. We flung our arms around each other. I don't know about Wally, but tears came to my eyes, making it difficult for me to see Maureen – my Maureen – as hand in hand, so tightly clasped together, we made our way to the Underground.

My dream of six years ago – a lifetime, it seemed – of having a girl on my arm had come true at last. I knew Maureen was the one for me when our hands came together; I had this elated feeling, that she felt as I did.

From that moment my life was about to begin, really begin. With God's help I survived the dangerous days and later, God willing, I will tell you of the more peaceful times.

The games we played

OI JIMMY KNACKER

'Oi Jimmy Knacker' was an East End street game of the 1930s, although in other parts of London it was known as 'Hi Jimmy Knacker'. In Croydon it was called 'Bury the Barrel', in Kirkcaldy it was 'Cuddy's Wecht', 'Mountikitty' on Tyneside, 'Bumberino' in South Wales and 'Pomperino' in Cornwall. In the Vnukour district of Moscow the game was known as 'Slona', and in Italy as 'Il cavallo lungo' ('the long horse'). A version of it is played in Turkey where it is known as 'Uzun Eshell' ('long donkey'), while in New York it is 'Johnny on the Pony'. It has even been seen in India and Japan.

Of all the street games this is the one that is readily remembered, possibly because it was the toughest, the one in which players were most frequently injured, and the one that required the greatest amount of stamina!

Two sides were chosen, and it was best to get the heftiest lads on your side. A boy known as the 'cushion' stood with his back to the lamp post, railings or whatever. The next in the team stooped down, placing his head in the cushion's stomach and holding on to his waist. The next boy in the team put his head under the second boy's legs and gripped his thighs, then the rest of the team did likewise. The 'horse' was then complete.

The other team was the 'jumping' team, who took it in turns to run across the street and jump on to the horse. Usually the best jumper in the team went first, for he had to endeavour to vault as far as he could along the horse, to enable the rest of his team to get on. Now all safely on the horse they sang a ditty, the E13 version of which was:

'Oi Jimmy Knacker, one, two, three,
One, two, three.
Oi Jimmy Knacker is got a flea,
Is got a flea.'

This was repeated three or four times. The team that won was the one that kept all its feet from touching the ground while perched on the horse's back during the singing of the ditty. For its efforts that team got another go.

A team also won if the horse collapsed under its weight. Of course, the 'jumping' team helped to bring this about by wriggling and bringing their combined weight to bear on the weaker part of the horse. If this happened, the riders all cried out 'Weak horses, weak horses, weak horses', then everyone chased across the street to the opposite pavement to start all over again.

Adapted from Children's Games in Street and Playground (Oxford University Press), © Iona and Peter Opie 1969

No Head For Heights

A J 'Bob' Kimberley

'Oh, come on, Ken!' Bobby called up the stairs. 'Johnny will be here soon, and we don't want to be late, and where's your pump, cos I want to pump up your tyres.'

Mum intervened. 'It's in the cupboard under the stairs.'

'What's it doing in there? It should be on his bike.'

I hastily got into my shorts, pulled my socks up, got into my shoes and hurried downstairs.

'Crikey,' I heard Bobby say, 'it's covered in coal dust!' – together with other odds and ends, as that was where we kept the coal!

'Oh, give it here, I'll dust it off. Your breakfast's on the table, Ken, have a wash,' Mum said, adding, 'Our Bob's not very pleased with you today, so you'd better keep out of his way.'

'Not much chance of that!' I thought. We were off on a three-day bike ride, 'across the water', as our Grandad used to say. There was a knock at the door as I gulped down the last of my breakfast.

'Shan't be long, John, I'm just waiting for our kid.' They both had their haversacks on their backs and Bob was fixing my waterproof cape on to my saddlebag. I had a junior Hercules roadster, while Bob and Johnny had Hercules racers, with dropped handlebars and three-speed gears. They had been mates since their early Cave Road Junior School days, and went on to Plaistow Secondary, where they had recently matriculated. Johnny was going off to Reading University, hoping to become a teacher, and after the holidays Bobby was off to find a job in commercial art – he was smashing at painting and drawing!

Mum helped me on with my small haversack. 'Be careful on the roads and do as Bobby says.'

She stood on the doorstep and with a wave we were off to Tilbury to get the ferry across

'...Bob and Johnny had Hercules racers, with dropped handlebars and three-speed gears.'

the river to Gravesend, Bob in front, me in the middle and Johnny Sullivan following, just to make sure I didn't lag behind.

It was cloudy and overcast when we wheeled our bikes down the gangway on to the ferry at Tilbury.

'I borrowed our Dad's box camera, hoping we can take a few snaps, Bob,' said Johnny.

'What about that Johnny!' I said excitedly, as a big cargo ship sailed close by with her giant propeller turning slowly as it headed downstream, unloaded now and high up out of the water. 'SS *Panama*' was written in large letters across her stern and dark faces waved to me as I waved to them.

'Oh, 'urry up, Johnny, else you'll miss her!'

Johnny fiddled with the case and at long last got the Brownie camera out and took his snap of the SS Panama.

We pushed our bikes up the narrow streets to Gravesend High Street. Bob and John were members of the YHA, but being under 12 I wasn't. We got back on our bikes and as we did so Bob put his arm around my shoulder. 'Sorry I snapped your head off this morning, kid. We've got about 30 miles to go –

the youth hostel's near Faversham. Sure you'll be all right?' he asked anxiously.

'Course I will, Bob, course I will.'

'Give us a shout when you want a break, promise?'

'OK,' I answered.

We stopped on the bridge across the River Medway, and out came John's box camera. 'Sit on the parapet,' he said to Bob and me. 'Give us a smile then!' Then Bob took one of John and me. 'Can I take one of you two?' I asked. The two schoolmates sat together and I took my first photograph.

Just across the bridge we stopped at a 'good pull-up for carmen'. After a Tizer, a cheese sandwich and a Milky Way we set off for a youth hostel. It was 3 o'clock. 'Not bad going, Johnny,' said Bobby, adding, 'You all right, Ken?'

'Course I am.'

With Johnny in the lead we set off on the last 20 miles or so. It was just 6 o'clock when Johnny shouted, 'It's just up the road – I can see the YHA signboard.'

My legs felt like jelly but I was as pleased as punch that I'd made it. We wheeled our bikes up the gravel path to the cottage, and John helped me off with my haversack.

The old man said, 'Follow me – the dormitory's round the back.' It

'Oh, 'urry up, Johnny, else you'll miss her!'

was an old barn with a thatched roof. 'Put your bikes under that there lean-to – don't allow no bikes in the dormitory.' He opened the door and pointed to the rows of neatly made-up beds 'You're the first in – take yer pick. The wash house and loos are across the yard, the cook house is in the lean-to at the back of the cottage, supper's sharp at 6 till 7 o' clock, don't be adrift else you'll miss it. Breakfast 7 till 8.'

He pointed to an open book on a makeshift desktop. 'Sign in – full name and address, please.' He asked to see Bob and John's YHA cards.

After supper – I forget what it was – 'We're going for a stroll round the village, kid – you coming?'

'OK,' I said, reluctantly. The tiny village boasted a church, the tower being covered in scaffolding and boards with ladders up to the very top.

'Look at that, John, you could take some smashing photos from up there.'

'Oh crikey, not up there,' I thought, as I was scared stiff of heights, but never let on to anybody! While Bob and Johnny would dive off the high diving board in the baths at Balaam Street, I would jump in at the 3-foot end!

We pushed open the big wooden gate, wheeled our bikes up the gravel path and leaned then against the scaffolding, Bob saying, 'Keep an eye on the bikes, kid.' I was only too willing to do so as they made their way up the ladders. I looked away as they both reached the very top,

'...Bob and Johnny would dive off the high diving board in the baths...'

glancing up again to see Johnny sitting astride the parapet taking his snaps, with Bob pointing out the best of the views! He looked down and waved – I made a poor effort of waving back. I sat on the crossbar of my bike and looked beyond the gravestones and a low brick wall.

'Oh, crikey!' I thought. 'Here comes the local "bluebottle",' as I saw his head and shoulders above the wall. I turned around and fiddled about with my saddlebag, hoping he hadn't noticed me. It wasn't to be, for minutes later I heard the crunch of his boots on the gravel path.

'Hello, my lad. What's going on then? What are you up to in here?'

'Well, er, we had a puncture,' I said, telling a white lie.

'What, the three of you? Cos there's three bikes 'ere. Where's your mates, then?' he asked. Daft me, I inadvertently looked up, and the bobby's eyes followed mine. 'Who's that?' he asked.

you to do
a few odd
jobs for them
about the place, but
thankfully he didn't
and after breakfast we
were on our way home.

The sun had gone down as we rode down the Barking Road, and we left Johnny at the Greengate, as he lived on the other side of Pelly Road bridge.

I felt pleased with myself as I rode next to Bob down Dongola Road, with him saying to me, 'Don't tell Mum about us climbing that scaffolding, Ken.'

'Course I won't.'

'It's my brother and his mate taking snaps,' I replied.

'I'll give 'em "taking snaps" when they get down here!' he exploded. Thankfully Bob and Johnny made it safely down, into the arms of the 'bluebottle'.

'Daft young fools! Don't you realise you could have broken your silly necks up there?'

'We didn't do any damage, Officer,' they both explained.

'Damage!' he exploded. 'The only damage you could have done was to yourselves! Where are you from?' he asked.

'London,' they replied.

'Oh, smart Alecs from up the smoke, eh?' he said with a grin, adding grudgingly, 'I admire your pluck, anyway, so off you go and stay on the ground when you're taking snaps in future!'

He closed the wooden gate behind us and we pedalled off as fast as we could.

We spent another night at the Youth Hostel. Sometimes wardens would ask

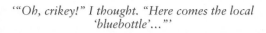
"Oh, crikey!" I thought. "Here comes the local 'bluebottle'…"

"I'll give 'em 'taking snaps' when they get down here!"

Mum was relieved to see us. 'There's hot water in the kettle so you can have a good wash,' she said, adding, 'Looks to me as if you need it, the pair of you. What's all that stone dust and rust on your shorts, Bob?' Bob made out not to hear, and I went into the scullery for a wash.

'I've made your favourite dinner!' she called. 'Toad in the hole, and spotted dick for afters.'

'There's no place like home!' I thought.

A. J. 'Bob' and Christine Kimberley on their wedding day

POSTSCRIPT:

A. J. 'Bob' Kimberley volunteered for the RAF, got his wings and flew fighter-bombers, proving again that he had a head for heights!

John Sullivan went on to become a teacher in Liverpool, but he was dismayed to be passed unfit for military service at the outbreak of the Second World War.

Personal recollection...

Bob flew through the air with the greatest of ease 300-400 mph in the RAF. As ever I kept my feet on terra firma during WWII, well not quite terra firma but on many oceans around the world, steaming at a steady 12 knots.

Ken Kimberley

The Woolwich Free Ferry

Anthony P Stanley
Tennessee USA

It was always an exciting day to take the tram down Woolwich way
And look over Beckton's drab, swampy fields, and gas works sooty grey.
For the likes of us it was but a penny fare,
From a gruff conductor who gave us both a growl and a glare.
On through Gallions and Royal Docks, delayed sometimes as a ship took the locks.

Gazing up at row upon row of monster tall cranes that reached into holds, cargo-full
Of every conceivable commodity of God's green earth, lumber, copra, rubber and wool.
Onward the tram rattles, bell clanging, through streets dressed in soot, dust and grime,
But clean scrubbed doorsteps, and shabby lace curtains of a long-gone time...
And on the final turn, sharp left, the horrendous screech of tortured steel,
And we feel the vibration through every Sheffield-built wheel,
But already we are looking out, thrilling to the sight of the day,
The Thames in its glory; windswept, choppy, cold and grey.
Impatiently jumping, running fast: 'The ferry's in! Here at last!'

We board the ferry with a proprietary air, like
braggart seadogs of the Spanish Main,
As we mount the gangplank, and feel the first
vibration and certain thrill again,
Even though it is but the high-pitched roar of a
generator that deafens.
We make our way to the main engine site where
mighty pistons are still,
Awaiting the jangle of telegraph that signals the
Captain's will,
And engineers heave great levers to loose the power
As, slow but sure, the great arms plunge down,
down, hissing, crashing,
And the whole ship begins to vibrate, echoing,
shaking, water splashing,

Foul-smelling mud creaming grey and dirty spuming yellow,
And amid the noise a strident voice has bellowed, 'Cast off!'

Great eye-bolts are manhandled from their bollards and thrown,
And as the hull grinds hard against the wood facing, a creaking groan,
But the pistons, synchronised, are plunging and lifting,
In a rhythm that carries one's heart upward with a surging thrill,
And all around is the magic odour of hot oil and steam,
Hot draughts, drumming and vibration; one must loudly shout,
And smile, and nod, each to the other, 'This is what it's all about!'

And now, breaking the mesmerising spell of rhythmic piston,
no time to bide,
Already we are well away, even in midstream – time to go topside!
Running, shouting, laughing, enjoying every moment of our young life,
Without a single care or thought of the real world's hard times and strife,
Dodging among the tight-packed trucks and delivery vans
from far and near,
And stopping for a moment to try and get a glimpse of Gallions Pier.
'Tug on the port quarter!' Jimmy shouts – always the cocky wag! –
As the tow draws near, four barges laden down heavy with acrid coke slag.
Then we hear the insistent clang of the bridge telegraph,
And in a moment the powerful vibrations lessen by half
As the helm heads in, slow ahead, to ease gently into berth.
The crossing completed, a job well done – and the very best show of our very young
lives.

At the time of writing it is still possible to travel by paddle steamer aboard
The Waverley *the only sea going paddle steamer in the world.*
For further details *visit the Waverley Excursions web site*
*at: **www.waverleyexcursions.co.uk***
or write to:
Waverley Excursions
Waverley Terminal
Anderston Quay,
Glasgow
G3 8HA

The original memoir from:

oi' Jimmy Knacker

Waiting for the tram to Wanstead Flats, Eddy said, 'I haven't a penny for the fare today.'

'Nor 'ave I,' said Albie.

'Well, what's the use of waiting here then?' the rest of us exclaimed.

'I know,' I said. 'Let's go to Woolwich. We can ride on the ferry cos it's free.' The trees and the ponds on the Flats were quickly forgotten as we all set off for Woolwich. Hurrying past the soap and gas works at Becton we held our noses. Cor, what a pong!

Shortly after, poking up amongst the chimney-pots, we could see ships' masts and brightly painted funnels. Cranes, like fingers, pointed up to the sky above the roof-tops, and instead of the soap factory we could smell Old Father Thames. We forgot the long walk in our excitement, hurrying around the last corner.

'Look, the ferry's in!' we all shouted. 'Hurry up – we don't want to miss it.'

With that there was a rush for the gangway. All out of breath, we decided that we would go up by the paddle-wheel first and go down and see the wonders of the engine room on the return trip. We climbed up beside it.

'Oi, you lads down there! Mind you behave or I'll have you ashore.'

'Aye-aye, Cap'n,' answered cheeky Albie Gibbs.

The view took our breath away – ships and boats of all shapes and sizes as far as our eyes could see, screeching seagulls, and sails. Oh, this was lots more fun than Wanstead Flats!

'Look, I bet those bobbies are after Doctor Fu Manchu down at Limehouse,' said Alf, as a river police launch sped by. Boom, boom, boom – the paddle-wheel began to turn and the water frothed up below us as we set off for distant shores. And as Grandad used to say, 'across the water' was like being in a foreign land, 'cos they don't even speak the King's English across there.'

Personal recollections...

Although I lived in Canning Town I am familiar with Plaistow, the Greengate public house and Balaam Street. I was evacuated to Somerset on 1 September 1939, and after three years I came north. My memory is so very clear about the Woolwich Ferry – it was a real pleasure to go back and forth, and I used to go to the Dockland Settlement and Rathbone Street Market.

Iris Yates, an East Ender

We would as kids, go down inside and watch the huge pistons going back and forth, my father would say '"you'll have to have a passport if you want to go ashore over there"'

Terry Ward

The Woolwich Ferry Paddle Steamers

Paddle steamers were once a common sight on the rivers and seas around Britain and are for the most part fondly remembered by those who travelled on them.

The paddle steamer reigned supreme on the Woolwich services for more than 50 years, there being seven in all:

Gordon	(built 1888) (a)
Duncan	(built 1888) (a)
Hutton	(built 1893) (a)
Squires	(built 1922) (b)
Gordon (2)	(built 1922) (b)
Will Crooks	(built 1930) (c)
John Benn	(built 1930) (c)

The vessels were named, respectively, after the following famous people: General Gordon (of Khartoum fame), Colonel Francis Duncan, Charles Hutton, William James Squires, William Crooks and Sir John Benn.

For the more technically minded, the specifications of the seven vessels were:

Length:	(a) 64ft, (b) and (c) 172ft
Breadth:	(a) 60ft, (b) and (c) 62ft
Draught:	(a) 4ft, (b) 4ft 6in, (c) 4ft 9in
Tonnage:	(a) 490, (b) and (c) 625
Speed:	8 knots
Capacity:	1,000 passengers, up to 20 vehicles
Builders:	(a) R. H. Green, except *Hutton*, built by W. Simons & Co Ltd, (b) and (c) Samuel White & Co Ltd

Suggested further reading:
Whites of Cowes
(Silver Link Publishing Ltd,
ISBN 1 85894 157 8)

Personal recollections...

I remember the run through Woolwich Tunnel, and back on the ferry, Wanstead flats, the park and Bush Wood, and the cinema and the baths at the YMCA in Greengate Street; also, being older, the illuminated tram that ran through West Ham, and when the 'Hammers' lost to Bolton Wanderers 2-1 at the first Cup Final at Wembley.

We also took advantage of the sixpence-all-day on the tram, a 65 to Bloomsbury, round the British Museum, then the Underground tram from Kingsway to the Embankment, the 38 to Borstal Woods, and back over on the ferry.

J. J. Blatchford

Kids get bored today – why? After school we went to West Ham Park with our football to get chased by 'Parkie' for playing on his cricket pitch. Otherwise it was St Georges Road, Strone Road, Katherine Road, past the Trebor sweet works, down Derby Road to Plashet Park; other times via East Ham Town Hall, walking on via the dock area to the Woolwich Ferry, a few trips across the free ferry, a walk through the tunnel (now closed), then home.

N. E. Wheeler

Characters we met

THE COFFEE STALL
Once a common feature in the suburban streets of Britain's towns and cities. These havens which offered a warming drink on a cold night, were a meeting point for all sorts of characters. The friendly face behind the counter would be a source of local information - ranging from directions to 'hot tips' and from the latest football results to the state of the nation!

THE NIGHT WATCHMAN
What better way to while away time on a cold Winter's evening than to make friends with the night watchman - the roaring coke in the brazier would be hard to resist, and the tales that would be told made for an enlightening evening for young and old alike.

THE ENGINE DRIVER
'Every boy wants to be a train driver' was an often stated expression! Certainly the footplate was a magnet for young boys - the lucky few would be invited aboard for a fleeting glimpse of life on the tracks.

OLD PARKY
As fast as he swept up it seemed, the faster the leaves would fall or the litter would accumulate! In winter he would be the obvious target for our snowball fights - threats of visiting the headmaster might stem the flow for at least a short respite. Park keepers were a feature of Britain's town and city parks back in those days, when they were so much more a focal point of entertainment.

The Evacuation

Alf Barrett remembers his adventure to Somerset

My Dad gave me a hug, saying, 'It won't be for too long, Alf,' adding, 'Now, don't forget to write as soon as you can – Mum's packed a writing pad, envelopes and lots of stamps with your things, so promise us to write.'

'Of course I will, Dad, course I will.' I stood at the door and he turned and waved to me as he went off to work at Bow. I remembered just in time to wish him a happy birthday.

As I went back into the kitchen Mum was holding back her tears. I went up to my bedroom, taking one long last look round and fingering through my picture cards in the cabinet that

Dad had specially made for me. From the wireless came the announcement again that children in the London area must report to their schools today, 1 September, with their gas masks and all the items on the list that had been handed to us some weeks before.

My mate Chas Mount and I thought it would be a big adventure and a bit of a skylark to go far off into the countryside, so we had persuaded our parents to sign the form saying that they were willing for us to do so. After all, the furthest we had ever been on a train before was Southend-on-Sea, just 30 miles away! Seeing Mum holding back her tears, I found it hard for me to hold back mine, now the day had come.

'It was a sea of sad faces that assembled in front of Mr Tom Lethaby, our headmaster...'

There was a knock on the front door. My pal stood on the doorstep with a small suitcase, his gas mask in the now familiar cardboard box slung across his shoulder. 'Ready, Alf?' he asked.

Mum handed me my case and gas mask. She put on a brave face, and so too did I, because I didn't wish for Chas to see that the great adventure we had talked about for weeks didn't have the same appeal on this Friday morning, but deep   down I knew he thought as I did!

We wondered when we would see our parents, our cosy homes and all the familiar faces in our little corner of E13 again. It was a sea of sad faces that assembled in front of Mr Tom Lethaby, our headmaster, for whom we all had great respect. I looked up at the old school, thinking how even those dreaded arithmetic lessons weren't so bad after all. Oh, and how I would miss those Saturday mornings down at Prince Regent Lane, where we would gather round Mr Murray for our weekly game of football, be it against Rossetta Road, Holborn Road or Star Lane! I stopped daydreaming when old Lethaby called my name, Alfred Barrett, 'Here, Sir!' I answered.

He went down the long list, and there were not many absentees. It was a silent procession that made its way to Plaistow Station, passers-by giving us a wave as we were shepherded along by Mr Lethaby, Old Cohn, the history master, Mr Leithhead, our woodwork teacher, Miss Newman, the headmistress of the infant's school, and a young lady in a large halo hat (I think that's what they were called!).

As the Mums, those that were there, said their tearful goodbyes, we filed into the waiting District Line train. At Paddington Station the photographers were out in force: 'Give us a smile!' they shouted to us, and we all half-heartedly obliged. Little did we know that the next day Chas and I, along with our schoolmates, Mr Lethaby, Mr Cohn and Mr Leithhead, Miss Newman

'In the next field a flock of sheep were chewing at the lush green grass, at peace with the world.'

and Miss Halo-hat, would be featured in the *Daily Mirror*!

The Great Western train took us through the rolling countryside of the West Country – it seemed endless, the longest train journey I had ever taken in my life. It finally stopped at Taunton.

'Well lads,' Mr Lethaby said, 'we're now in lovely Somerset.' To us cockney kids it seemed like the ends of the earth! Buses took us to a tiny village about 5 miles from Taunton. The coach stopped to let 12 or so contented-looking fat cows cross the road, a small boy prodding them along with a long stick. He closed the gate to the farmyard and gave us a wave.

Miss Newman turned in her seat saying, 'There you are lads. They're off to be milked – that's where your daily bottle of milk comes from.'

In the next field a flock of sheep were chewing at the lush green grass, at peace with the world. It was late afternoon when we were herded into the village hall, the sun going down over the rooftops. 'Welcome to Somerset,' said a distinguished-looking old man with a row of medals pinned across his breast pocket.

Chas nudged me, saying, 'I bet he's an old colonel.'

The old gent went on, 'I'll get what I have to say over with as quickly as possible, eh? I appreciate you've all had a long and distressing journey. I must ask all those who are brothers and sisters, cousins or close relations to move to the far end of the hall.' There was a lot

of shuffling about, and eventually Chas and I, together with a few others, found ourselves standing alone.

I prayed that Chas and me would be kept together, but it wasn't to be. An hour later all the brothers and sisters were taken away by, it seemed, well-off-looking ladies. An elderly couple, Mr and Mrs Barnes, took me off, while Chas went in the opposite direction.

It was dark now as I accompanied my new 'carers' down the gloomy country lane to a tiny cottage, the like of which I had never seen before, except in pictures – no pavements, no streetlights. Mr Barnes lifted a flowerpot that concealed the front door key. Being reasonably

I accompanied my new 'carers' down the gloomy country lane to a tiny cottage

tall for my age I felt I had to duck under the low beam above the door. Holding firmly on to my suitcase and with my gas mask still over my shoulder, I followed them in. The oil lamps lit the small living room, a small log fire burned in the grate deep inside the inglenook fireplace. I noticed a clothes-line stretched across the far end of the room with some washing hanging up to dry. There wasn't much furniture about.

'You'll be wanting to get up to bed,' they both said, 'after that long journey from up there.'

'Oh yes please,' I answered. The wife lit a candle and said, 'Follow me, lad.'

Mrs Barnes opened a tiny door that

revealed a small flight of steps, and with head bent I followed her. The candle in its holder flickering in the draught as she opened another tiny door, and again with head bent low I followed her into my 'bedroom'. 'Suppose it's not what you've been used to, boy.' It certainly wasn't!

I endeavoured to look around myself in the gloomy darkness, relieved only by the flickering candle. It smelled of whitewash and damp straw! 'Where's my bed?' I asked myself. I stepped forward and tripped over a mattress that lay on the floor.

'Sorry we haven't a proper bed, dearie, but it'll do for the time being,' she said, adding, 'Anyway, you'll find it's nice and soft. I'll bring you up a nice cup of cocoa in a minute,' and she left me alone endeavouring to look around my new surroundings! I drank the cocoa that she brought up. 'I'll leave the candle up here, but make sure you put it out,' she emphasised to me.

I undressed and piled my clothes on the lone chair that stood beside the mattress. I put the candle out and looked out of the tiny latticed window into the darkness of the countryside thinking of Mum and Dad in far-away Plaistow. Was this the big adventure Chas and I had talked of some months ago? I wondered how he was getting on! 'Oh, what have I done?' I thought, and turned over on the mattress, tired out

now, pulling the blanket over me and thankfully soon falling asleep, dreaming that I'd scored the winning goal against Star Lane School!

I had tea and toast early next morning. 'There's more if you want it,' said Mrs Barnes. The Barneses looked after a large orchard close by. 'You can come with us if you wish, lad, or make yourself at 'ome here.'

Not wishing to be left alone I joined them in the orchard, doing this and that. The village looked more inviting in the morning sunshine. I wrote to Mum and Dad, saying that I was all right and hoped they were and gave them my address.

I walked up to the village shop that served as the Post Office among

'...with head bent low I followed her into my "bedroom"...'

other things. Charlie stood outside with some fellow evacuees and was thrilled to see our picture in the *Daily Mirror* that was in a rack outside.

'How you getting on, Chas?' I asked 'Oh, all right, Alf,' was all he had to say. I didn't tell him of my feelings in case he wrote home, knowing all too well that Mrs Mount would tell Mum how I felt! Efforts were being made to organise some school lessons for us, but it was proving difficult to integrate us into the local school. During the evening meal with the Barnes family I met their son, older than me. They made a point of saying that tomorrow, as on every Sunday, I would be expected to join them at the local chapel, and they looked shocked when I declined.

In Plaistow, when younger, I regularly attended Sunday School, but Mum and Dad always said that as long as I remained decent, honest, law-abiding and did unto others as I'd wish them to do to me, that would satisfy them and they couldn't ask for more. I explained this to the Barneses, but I could see by their faces that they remained unmoved, and from then on it proved more difficult for me to fit into their day-to-day family life.

In the early afternoons Chas and I and other known evacuees met up outside the village shop. There was a wireless set up on a crate of empty milk bottles. 'There is a special announcement,' the voice said, and the Prime Minister, Mr Chamberlain, went on to say that as he had received no reply from the German Chancellor, Herr Hitler, requesting that he withdraw the German Army from the Polish frontiers by 11am today, Sunday the 3rd of September, 1939, 'I must

'Charlie stood outside with some fellow evacuees and was thrilled to see our picture in the Daily Mirror...'

tell you that a state of war exists between the United Kingdom and British Empire across the seas. That is all.' All feeling downcast, we realised that an early return to our own homes looked unlikely!

I excitedly opened Mum's letter. They were all right and I was not to worry for them, she said. 'Your Aunt Rose with her young daughter has been evacuated to Wiltshire, about 50 miles from you.'

The second week, together with Chas and a few others from the old school, I found myself on a bus back to Taunton. At least we found that Taunton had a few home comforts – big shops, a picture palace, pavements and traffic lights, lots of people and, we thought, a bit more like home! We boarded

the bus for our return to the village, while the driver and conductor had a break in a nearby café. Of course, for a bit of fun, we ran up and down the empty bus, dinging the bell, but hastily returned to our seats when the driver climbed up into his cab.

'Where's the conductor?' we asked ourselves. Albie, always the most daring of us, dinged the bell and with that off went the bus, the driver unaware that the conductor had been left behind. A very cross driver demanded to know, 'Who rang the bell?' He was greeted with a stony silence. A few minutes later

a furious, flustered and out of breath conductor came chasing down the lane.

'What's the idea of going off without me?'

'It's those little London buggers!' explained the driver. 'We're in for some trouble with those little so-and-sos, you mark my words.'

Walking home down the village street I passed a grand-looking house set back down a gravel driveway. The door flew open and out ran two lads. One I recognised straight away as Dennis Pitney, but the smaller one I didn't know – we were in the same class down at Balaam Street. 'Watcha, Alf!' Dennis called out. 'This is me kid brother. Where you staying?'

'Oh, just up the lane.'

'Cor, you should see where we are! Talk about posh – they've got, er, a maid and someone who does all the cooking, haven't we, kid? You should see our bedroom, all to ourselves, and next door is our own bathroom, with a shower, first one I've ever seen! She's a lovely lady. Her old man, he's a major and is in France. Gotta dash, Alf – she's asked us to get her magazine from the Post Office. What's she call it, kid?' The small

'...off went the bus, the driver unaware that the conductor had been left behind...'

brother mumbled, '*Country Life.*' 'Never heard of it meself,' said Dennis. 'Look, she gave us five bob and told us to get some sweets for ourselves. See you later, Alf!' And they both ran off.

Walking home down the now familiar lane I turned the last corner and had another surprise, a lovely one, because coming out of the cottage was my Aunt Rose. Caring Aunt Rose had travelled 50 miles just to see me, just to see if I was all right. Mrs Barnes had asked her in, saying that I had gone off to Taunton, and made her a cup of tea.

'She's kind enough, Alf, so it seems, but I couldn't stay one night in there, and as for your bedroom, well, your Mum would have a fit if she saw it! The place gives me the creeps.'

'It's not too bad,' I replied.

'Oh, come on Alf, tell me another one! Look, I've got to dash, else I'll miss the bus in Taunton.' She gave me a big hug and a kiss and with a wave went off to get her bus.

Three or four days later I heard from Mum, saying that with a group of parents from Balaam Street School they had organised a coach trip to see us – just for the day, she added.

The great day arrived, Sunday 24 September, and we all anxiously awaited their arrival outside the village shop. Anxious Mums and Dads enquired of our well-being, though it was obvious from what Mum said that my Caring Aunt Rose had told Mum what she thought. 'You're coming back home with me, Alf. Go and collect your things from Mrs Barnes. Oh, and make sure you thank her for looking after you – don't forget now!'

I walked down the lane for the last time and explained to Mrs Barnes that Mum wanted me to go back with her. 'Oh, I understand. I wouldn't wonder that your Mum and Dad are missing you.' She reached up to her clothes-line and took my newly washed shirt down. ''Fraid it's a bit damp, but wrap it up in yer towel and it'll be all right.' I thanked her, as Mum had asked me, and shook her weathered old hand, then with a last wave I turned back to the village.

We found Charlie, whose mother had asked Mum to bring him back too, and it was two happy lads that squeezed in beside Mum for the long journey back home. I can say now it was one of the

'*...it was one of the happiest days of my life when we got off the coach in Plaistow Broadway.*'

happiest days of my life when we got off the coach in Plaistow Broadway. The blackout was in force but the pavements were still there and all the familiar places, just as I had left them.

A relieved Dad opened the door. It was wonderful to see him again, but the joy of it all lasted just 12 months or so – in September 1940 we were packing up again, collecting what was left of our belongings and leaving Plaistow, E13, for good. We had been bombed out!

Postscript

Just before Christmas Mum said, 'I'll send old Mrs Barnes a card, Alf, cos she did her best for you.' She wrote our new address on the inside – perhaps she would answer it. She never did.

However, in the June after Dunkirk a short note came, addressed to Mum, asking of my well-being, and saying that life continued as ever in the village. It ended, 'Alf may have remembered my son Alfred. He was wounded and taken prisoner. He was in the Territorial Army and went to France shortly after Alf left us.'

'...in September 1940 we were packing up again... We had been bombed out!'

Dolly gets a soaking

Nellie Amelia Lovell

Mum helped me up into my Dad's cart so that I could sit beside him, saying "don't forget you have your best dress on, you'll probably come home smelling of Brussel sprouts and bannanas". "Oh don't fuss the child mum" and with a slight pull on the reigns we were off, Dolly stepping out into Westborne Grove.
" Can I be a greengrocer when I grow up?" I asked, "greengrocer you, we've better things in mind for you my luv, 'sides it's a mans work, not for ladies, that would give 'em all a laugh down the 'Garden' at 5 o'clock in the morning that's for sure." "Where we going Dad?"

Dolly was stepping smartly down Church Street now. "Oh the usual Saturday rounds, best day of the week for me luv - all the posh places off the High Street." "What's posh Dad?" - "You know luv - well off, rich like." "Don't they go shopping for their greengroceries" I asked. "No fear luv, they only go shopping in Harrods and such places, wouldn't be seen dead, carrying a bag of tatters and sprouts, mind you that's 'ow I like it!
We joined a queue of other carts and buses " always digging up the roads, it's those 'Paddys' looking for gold I reckon me luv." As we passed by I glanced down the hole, as I did so a great big fountain of water leapt up - poor Dolly disappeared under it! Dolly reared up and galloped off, I fell back amongst Dad's potatoes and vegetables -. "hang on tight Nellie she is going to take some stopping!" Everything scattered out of the way. Its those blinking 'Paddys' they've hit a water main. The cart rocked to and fro, Dad's vegatables flew all over the road. A brave policeman ran from the watching crowds, grappled with Dolly's reins - his boots dragging the cobble stones. Dad lifted me off the cart - an exhausted policeman saying '"You alright little girl?"' I buried my head into Dad's coat - holding back my tears as I looked down at my dress. Dad thanked the policeman for his brave deed, "Here you are little girl here's a penny, buy yourself a nice big lollipop"

A night to forget

by Elizabeth Doris Wilkins

'Sleep well, ladies,' the cheeky conductor called to us as we got off the bus at the Abbey Arms. 'Not much chance of that,' my friend said as we crossed the Barking Road, and made our way down New Barn Street on this cold winter night. I worked in Mare Street, Hackney, and waiting at the bus stop in the blackout we had started to chat, and this became a regular thing as she worked close by me.

'See you tomorrow, Doris,' she said as she opened her bag and searched for her key in the darkened street.

'Live in hopes,' I said, as I hurried down New Barn Street, and turned into Denmark Street. Here and there an offending chink of light escaped through not tightly closed curtains, and the warmth of the kitchen fire welcomed me as I walked down the passage at home. Dad, Billy and Owen were sitting around the cheerful fire, Dad was reading the paper, and the wireless was on.

'Here you are, Dot, this'll warm you up,' said Mum as she put my dinner on the table. 'The others have had theirs.'

'Thanks, Mum.'

'Had a good day?' she asked.

'Oh, all right – 'course, we can never do enough for old Lill Spanton.'

Dad put his paper down. 'Better get ready for the night, I suppose.' He went into the scullery and got his bits and

pieces together. Finishing dinner, I went upstairs and did likewise, making sure I collected my bag of knitting. Two flasks of tea and the box of biscuits were on the kitchen table. 'Perhaps they won't be over tonight,' said my brother hopefully. 'I wouldn't bet on it,' replied his mate Owen.

Owen was proved right an hour later. As Dad marshalled us all down the garden to the Anderson shelter, he had a last look round the kitchen, put the

'...Dad drew the heavy old curtain over the Anderson opening, and we sat down in our now usual places.'

fireguard in front of the fire and joined us in the shelter. Mum had lit the candles, Dad drew the heavy old curtain over the Anderson opening, and we sat down in our now usual places: Mum and I at the back, Billy on one side facing Owen, who sat opposite, and Dad as always with his back to the curtain. I started my knitting; I wonder how many pairs of socks I've knitted for the soldiers, I asked myself. Billy and Owen were asking each other whether it was to be the Navy, Army or Air Force when their time came to join up. Mum chimed in, 'Perhaps it will be all over before you have to go.' How many mothers were thinking the same thing, I wondered.

I sat there with my thoughts of long-ago pre-war days, out dancing three nights a week – Balaam Street baths in the winter time, Poplar Town Hall or the Winter Gardens at East Ham. Look at us now sitting here night after night in this hole in the ground! Oh well, I expect it could be worse, I thought!

'Hold on a minute, Dot,' Dad said. I stopped knitting, and the click, click of my needles ceased. Yes, we all heard it, that unmistakable 'throb, throb, throb' of the Jerry bombers growing louder with each passing second. Dad got up and pushed aside the curtain enough for him to squeeze through.

'"Billy, Doris, Owen! The house is on fire!"'

'Don't go out there, Will,' Mum said. 'Oh, you know he likes to have a look round to see what's going on,' I said. 'Crump, crump' went the AA guns. Dad stepped down into the shelter as the shrapnel rained down. 'Swish, swish, swish' – we all cocked our ears at the unfamiliar sound. Again Dad was on his feet, and went out, closing the curtain behind him.

'Billy, Doris, Owen! The house is on fire!' we heard him call out. 'Bring up the buckets by the back door!' – he kept them there for such an emergency. 'Owen, run across to the ARP post in the school yard opposite and tell 'em what's happened!'

I saw Bill chase upstairs with his bucket. I followed, but in the dark I

forgot Bill's bike in the passage – too late. I caught my foot in the protruding pedal. 'Oh, Billy's rotten old b— bike – why does he keep it in the passage,' were my thoughts as my face crashed down on the handlebars and the bucket flew out of my hand, shooting its contents, muddy coal dust, up the passage towards the front door, just as Owen, with a stirrup pump over his shoulder, came in with the ARP man.

'Oh, Doris, you've brought in the

'I caught my foot in the protruding pedal.'

wrong bucket,' I heard him call out. I was too dazed and shocked to worry about right and wrong buckets!

Dad came downstairs minutes later, saying, 'It's all right, Liz, I smothered it with some blankets and Bill's bucket of water and it burned itself out in the fireplace!'

With relief we heard the 'All Clear'. 'Oh, Will,' said Mum as dad put the lights on, 'look at the state of my passage. I only washed and polished it this morning!'

'Don't worry, Liz. We were lucky – make us a cup of tea!'

'Lucky?' I thought. I glanced in the mirror and between the cuts and bruises and cut lips I didn't recognise myself. 'Oh Mum, look at the state of my face. I can't go out looking like this!'

But I did, and went to work a few hours later, but our forelady sent me straight back home. 'Oh Doris, go straight to the doctors!' I did and stayed at home for 14 days.

In doing so I missed the terrible accident at Bethnal Green Underground station – the siren sounded during the rush hour and as a result of the rush and panic to get underground many were killed in the ensuing chaos.

Proud and pleased

Ernie Bright

I had reason to feel a bit proud of myself at 14½, having been out at work for six months, but now handing over to Mum my weekly wage packet of 15 shillings, Mum keeping 10 shillings and handing me back the remaining two half-crowns for myself.

From this I had saved enough to buy my first sports jacket and grey flannels from the Fifty Shilling Tailors, and my matching tie I had 'borrowed' from my eldest brother. I was pleased with myself because these were the first new clothes I had ever bought!

It was Saturday afternoon and I was off to the 'Kinema' down West Ham Lane to see *On Your Toes* starring Alan Jones, a favourite American film star.

'...I had saved enough to buy my first sports jacket and grey flannels from the Fifty Shilling Tailors...'

It was a warm mid-September afternoon as I handed my sixpence through the hole in the glass partition of the pay box.

Pushing aside the curtain at the doorway, I made my way down to the 'sixpennies' at the very front, passing the more expensive 'two bobs'. Looking about me, I sensed that there wasn't more than a few dozen people in the 'Kinema' that Saturday afternoon, most probably out shopping at Stratford or down at Green Street Market.

'Seconds later the old lady landed in my lap, and her husband was spread-eagled across the adjoining seats.'

I sat in the middle of the second row; an old couple were the only occupants in the front row. The lights dimmed and Popeye and Olive Oyl came rowing across the screen – everybody loved Popeye and his mates. This was followed by the more serious news of the day, showing old Churchill reviewing shore defences on the South Coast, with his usual fat cigar clenched between his teeth, his walking stick and the famous 'V' sign. Our King was shown chatting to Dunkirk survivors, while the Duke of Kent was making his way along a line of the 'Famous Few' at an airfield in the Home Counties. We all felt a bit more secure now that the threat of invasion had passed!

Was that thunder that I heard? Alan Jones suddenly became lost under what looked like a flurry of snowflakes, then, with a roar like an express train, Alan Jones and bits of the 'silver screen' flew left, right and centre. I was lifted out of my sixpenny seat into the front row of the two bobs. Seconds later the old lady landed in my lap, and her husband was spread-eagled across the adjoining seats.

'Where's my Fred?' she moaned. 'I've lost my glasses – I can't see.'

'Fred's all right,' I managed to blurt out. 'He's sitting next to me.'

With an effort Fred scrambled up. 'You all right, Alice?' – not knowing where Alice was. I assured Fred that Alice was all right, and between us we pulled her off my lap. Through the dust and haze torchlights were dancing all around the

'Between
us Fred and
I helped his
Alice out on to the
pavement...'

of tea, won't we, love?' I just hoped their home was still there when they got to it! I left them to it and turned down West Ham Lane. I looked down at my shoes. 'Crikey! Look at the state of me!' I was covered in brick and plaster dust, mixed with what was left of my choc-ice. 'So much for my new sports jacket and flannels!' I thought.

I hurried over the bridge at Plaistow station and heard them saying, 'Canning Town and Custom House ain't 'arf copped it!' I could see for myself how true this was, for in the darkening September evening the sky beyond Trinity Church was now a crimson

remains of our 'Kinema', and caring usherettes helped us over the debris-strewn gangway.

By now firemen and rescue-workers were looking for the less fortunate. Between us Fred and I helped his Alice out on to the pavement, and amid the chaos Alice gave me a big hug. 'Thanks, lad.'

'Will you be all right now?' I asked.

'We're only five minutes walk from home, and we'll have a nice cup

'I hurried over the
bridge at Plaistow
station...'

'"Oh Ernest! Where 'ave you been? Look at the state of you!' Ma said.'

glow. I ran down Plaistow High Street and turned into Florence Road, and with relief saw that everything looked as I had left it a few hours before. As I did so the 'All Clear' sounded.

I turned the key in the lock of number 27, opened the door and hurried down the passage. It was like any other Saturday evening; they were all sitting round the table having tea.

'Oh Ernest! Where 'ave you been? Look at the state of you!' Ma said. Laurence, whose tie I had 'borrowed' earlier, said, 'Look at my best tie! What 'ave you done with it?'

Blackie, our cat, stretched himself out on the arm of the sofa, yawned and went back to sleep.

The games we played

CONKERS

This traditional street game is played the length and breadth of the country.

According to the *Shorter Oxford English Dictionary* the game was played originally with snail shells, which provides the origin of the name. 'Conker' is a dialect name for a snail shell, probably related to 'conch', which comes from the French and Latin.

The first recorded game of conkers was on the Isle of Wight in 1848, and was modelled on a 15th-century game played with hazelnuts, also known as cobnuts.

SOAP BOX DERBY

Not surprisingly, the soap box cart derives its name from the fact that it was made from a soap box; these were originally made from wood and provided a strong basis on which to build. The other essential ingredient

The World Conker Championships are held every year on the second Sunday in October on the village green at Ashton in Northamptonshire. Contestants are not allowed to use their own conkers; nuts are supplied for each game after being gathered and strung by the organisers. Each game lasts 5 minutes. If neither conker has broken, a shoot-out takes place. Each player has three sets of three hits and the one who lands most clean hits is the winner.

was an old pram or pushchair from which the axle and wheels could be utilised. Often referred to as 'trolleys', these machines were considered every bit as much of a status symbol as the 'dream cars' of today. Indeed, there was a very competitive spirit, not only in the racing of the carts, but also in their construction. Paint jobs and 'go-faster' stripes were very much the order of the day, and a suitable name completed the dream of the real racing car! In the days before widespread car ownership, back streets were ideal 'race tracks' and the passage of a car or delivery vehicle would be but a fleeting inconvenience. Even today the Soap Box Derby remains popular, particularly in the USA, and organised races, often linked to charity fund-raising, attract a dedicated following.

one that has defeated all-comers, the one that brings good luck whenever it is rolled – trickles ever closer to the mighty chasm that is the street drain, the mole-hole or the rabbit burrow!

KNOCKING DOWN GINGER

This game involves ringing a doorbell or knocking as loud as possible on a door knocker and running away as fast as possible to a 'safe' distance. The 'safe distance' is often used as part of a challenge whereby the participants, often referred to as 'rascals', endeavour to hide as close to the door as possible without being seen!

The next, and perhaps greatest, challenge is to wait a short time, to allow the owner to settle back into whatever they were doing, before once again knocking on the door!

The game has many names and variations and is often played by tying cotton thread on the door knocker and hiding first before pulling the thread.

MARBLES

It would be easy to describe marbles as the ultimate in traditional British street games. Certainly it has been played in streets, parks, gardens and school playgrounds for as long as anyone living today can remember. The precise rules of the game are something of a mystery, there being considerable variations on national, regional and local levels. Indeed, 'local' could be defined as neighbouring streets! The glass balls of recent times have been produced in a vast range of colours and many different sizes. As with most things to be found in the school playground, marbles have been swapped, collected, traded, lost, argued about and competed over with considerable enthusiasm! There have been endless leagues and championships, some lasting a matter of days, a school term or indeed over several years.

The game is not without its hazards. How many readers can recall those last agonising seconds as one's prize marble – the

Climb to the top

Leslie Barker

My grandparents were true East Enders, born within the sound of Bow Bells. Their forebears were publicans, so in the latter part of the 1800s and into the 1900s they followed the family tradition, serving ales and spirits from their pub, 'The Old House at Home' in Shadwell in the heart of London's Dockland. Grandmother met and wed Charlie Barker; when and how they met is lost in the pages of history, and in the time-honoured fashion of those days numerous sons and daughters followed.

My father, one of the sons, was born in 1889 and christened Albert Ernest Barker. He met his beloved Elizabeth Coombes, they became man and wife, and fathered a family of 11; sadly, as was often the case in those times, four of the children died at childbirth. Born in 1908, I was one of the fortunate ones who survived, and was christened Leslie Charles Barker, being the third eldest of the seven that lived.

Father was a skilled carcase-cutter in Smithfield, and for those times earned a good wage that enabled us to live in reasonable comfort at Barking on the eastern outskirts of London. Sadly for me, I wasn't a healthy lad, and a serious stomach ailment meant that I missed most of my early schooldays and was still attending a clinic in Barking in 1919.

I was, however, fortunate in having a mother and father who helped me with my early schooling at home – at least I mastered the 'three Rs', if nothing else.

In my early years my grandparents purchased another pub, 'The Beehive' at Bromley by Bow, opposite the Lusty works, makers of the famous Lloyd Loom furniture.

Come 1922, when I was 14, and healthier now, I got a job as an office boy in the counting house at Grace Sherwood & Heald in Barking, the

'...making tea for the seniors, filling the inkwells, and doing this and that – what all office boys did in those days.'

nationally known paint and distemper manufacturers, making tea for the seniors, filling the inkwells, and doing this and that – what all office boys did in those days. I was conscious of my lack of schooling, though, but was determined to keep up with the other lads and strived to better them.

Boys will be boys, and during the dinner break we would skylark about in the factory yards, something I had missed, having never experienced schooldays, as it were. It was a fine sunny day when we sat down amongst the empty barrels and drums in the yard, where we enjoyed a crusty cheese sandwich or something like. Gazing up at the tall chimney stack, we would guess how high it was – 40, 50, 60 feet? Oh no, 'course not – it's higher than that, we would argue.

'I'd like to climb up it,' somebody said.

'Dare you to!' we all shouted.

'I'll have a go,' I found myself saying.

'You?' they all said, laughing. 'Course you won't!'

'Bet you I will!' I heard myself saying again.

'We dare you to then.'

I had this overwhelming desire to prove to myself that I could do it, so off I went, up the short iron ladder to the roof of the boiler house, up the short iron ladder at the foot of the chimney, to the iron ladder set into the side of the chimney brickwork itself.

I looked down as I put my foot on to the first rung. There they all were, looking up at me. More determined now than ever, 'I'll show 'em,' I kept repeating to myself as I made my way up and up and up, stopping now and again to get my breath and to gaze over the rooftops of Barking and out to the low-lying mud flats that stretched way out to the River Thames. I stopped again and could see the ships and sailing barges making their way up and down the river, and the new Ford motor car factory that was reaching up to the sky and beyond to the distant hills across the river.

Looking down again, I was astonished to see the yard below was full of the factory hands pointing and gesturing up to me, and there was old Simpson, our office manager, with the rest of the office clerks among them.

I heard faintly at first the fire engine's bell, then it grew louder and louder. I saw a copper standing in the middle of the Barking Road holding up the trams and buses, horses and carts, enabling the engine to turn into our yard. I wondered what all the fuss was about! I could see the fire brigade officer surrounded by my office mates,

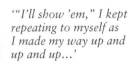

'"I'll show 'em," I kept repeating to myself as I made my way up and up and up…'

who were pointing up to me. Suddenly they all looked like midgets. Firemen now stood on the boiler house roof.

The big brass helmet shouted to me, 'Leslie – Leslie Barker! Can you hear me? Listen, lad, you've won your dare, do you hear me? Leslie, come down now. You've proved to us all you could do it, so be a good chap and come down now, do you hear me? You don't want us to come up after you, do you?'

'Cor, no fear!' I thought. 'They'll all think I can't climb down as well as climb up.' I had one last long look around over the rooftops of Barking and beyond. Taking my first step down the iron ladder, the brass hat called, 'There's no hurry, lad, take your time.' He caught hold of me as I put my foot on the boiler house roof. 'Good lad, good lad.' I believe he was more relieved to see me than I was to see him!

I stood in front of Old Simpson's desk. 'Young man, that was a very foolhardy thing to do. Promise me that you'll never ever attempt such a foolish act again.' He went on, 'I don't know what your mother and father will say when they get

'Firemen now stood on the boiler house roof.'

to hear of it, as I'm sure they will. Get into the kitchen,' he offered me a clothes brush, 'and have a good wash and brush down – you're covered in brick dust,' adding, 'You can have the rest of the day off.' And with half a smile he added, 'And don't be late for work in the morning.'

After this escapade, it was about this time that grandfather died – my memory fails me as to the year – followed soon after by my grandma. I was to learn later that while the pub at Shadwell prospered, 'The Beehive' at Bromley by Bow didn't. The 1920s brought difficult times. The promised 'land fit for heroes' after the Great War hadn't materialised, and the dole queues became longer as the Depression bit deeper and deeper.

'Stanley,' my eldest brother said, 'I overheard Mum and Dad saying that we may have to move to Bow.' 'What for?' I asked. 'Dunno – don't tell them I told you.'

'I stood in front of Old Simpson's desk.'

We were soon to learn, however, that the powers that be who were endeavouring to sort out grandma's affairs on her death found that all was not well – far from it. 'The Old House at Home' had to be sold, and 'The Beehive' at Bromley by Bow was losing money hand over fist. It was suggested that Dad and Mum take it on as a last resort in a desperate attempt to inject new life into it! They did so, but reluctantly, mainly because Dad had to leave his job in Smithfield.

A few months later, after leaving our home in Barking, 1924 found me pulling pints behind the bar in 'The Beehive', helping Dad with the cellar work and all the other routine pub work. I sensed that mother and father were far from happy in their new way of life – they were working desperately hard but customers became fewer and fewer as the Depression continued. Folks were finding it hard to put food in their families' mouths, let alone propping up our bar in 'The Beehive' at Bow.

The climax came in 1926, the year of the General Strike, bringing the great coalfields of the North and Wales to a standstill. London's docklands, as with all others, suffered the same fate.

At times I watched City workers manning buses and driving their colleagues to work. Angry strikers were kept at a distance by mounted police – the Army escorted food convoys from the East India Docks through silent and bitter strikers. Trade at 'The Beehive' became worse. I was scrubbing down the door step when I heard Dad say, 'Liz, I've had enough – if we carry on like this, what savings we've got will 'ave gone. I'm going up to Smithfield tomorrow, and if old Bill Thomas is still about I'll ask him for my old job back. I've heard that meat is still getting up to Smithfield.'

'Whatever you say, Charlie,' I heard Mum say.

Dad came back full of smiles. 'I can start whenever I want,' he told Mum. A few months later we left 'The Beehive' and moved into a small two-up-two-down in Chadwell Heath, and Dad went back to the work he was skilled at.

'...1924 found me pulling pints behind the bar in "The Beehive"...'

It was now 1928, and the huge LCC estates were being built at Dagenham and Becontree close by. I was fortunate to get a job with one of the contractors as a painter, although the only painting I ever did was creosoting yard after yard of wooden fences, returning home at night reeking of creosote. It was a job, and I had to accept the smell that went with it! But Mum knew that I wanted better things for myself.

'Leslie, there's a job going at that posh furniture store in Ilford High Road, Harrison Gibson's – they want a driver's mate.' The advert said to write to the Dispatch Foreman for an interview. I did so that very night, and was granted an interview on a Saturday afternoon.

Crikey, Mum was right when she said it was a posh place. It gleamed and sparkled, and the furniture and furnishings were of a kind that I had never seen before.

'You're a bit on the small side for a driver's mate, lad,' he said.

'I'm used to hard work,' I replied, relating my experiences in 'The Beehive' of the previous years.

'All right, lad, I'll give you a fortnight's trial – 7s 6d a week. Start on Monday

'...the only painting I ever did was creosoting yard after yard of wooden fences...'

looking smart and tidy, eh? Eight o'clock sharp.'

I couldn't get home to Chadwell Heath quick enough to tell them at home of my good fortune. I didn't wish to see another creosote brush in my whole life! Truth be known, even today if I pass a newly creosoted fence the smell takes me back 70 years or so. Mum handed me a stiff white collar. 'I'll find you two of your father's collar studs,

'Mum was right when she said it was a posh place. It gleamed and sparkled...'

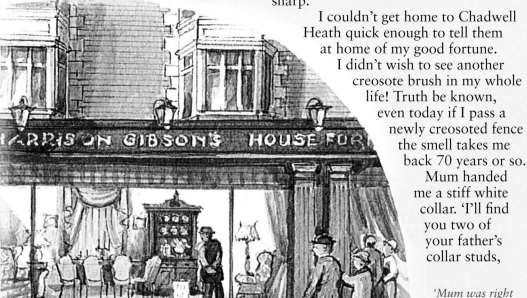

and borrow one of his ties, he won't miss them,' she said. She had polished my shoes so I could see my face in them, and my trousers had knife-like creases.

It was a confident Leslie Barker who walked into Harrison Gibson's dispatch department on Monday at 8am sharp.

It was pandemonium – vans being loaded, and wardrobes, sideboards, sofas, chairs and tables standing about, waiting their turn.

I recognised the Dispatch Foreman, bending over a sideboard. 'Harry!' he called out, 'get a polisher out here, I'm not 'appy with this 'ere top, and a cabinetmaker – one of the drawers wants easing.' He moved on to a luxurious-looking sofa. A driver in a brown overall pointed to the arm: 'There's some loose cotton on this arm, guv.'

'Get an upholsterer to look at it. Don't be put off by them saying they're too busy – I want somebody down 'ere now.' He looked up at me. 'What do you want?'

'Er, er, you told me to report to you this morning,' I said.

'What for?'

'I'm the new driver's mate,' I replied.

'Ah, yes. Willy 'ere's your new sparring partner,' he called out above the hustle and bustle. Willy appeared from behind his van, a big chap. 'He'd make two of me,' I thought. 'Get this young man sorted out with a coat, clocking-on card and the rest of it, right?' Then the guv'nor, as they called him, was off to attend to more important things than the new driver's mate, it seemed.

It was a nervous Leslie Barker who helped Willy let down the tailboard in the drive of a big house in Woodford. He put a small box on the ground that acted as a step. 'Right, son, you take that end. I'll go first, just keep it upright and there'll be no problems.'

There wasn't, much to my surprise.

'Off you go and knock at the door – tell

"'Right, son, you take that end. I'll go first, just keep it upright…'"

'em HGs are 'ere with a delivery.'

The day flashed by. My problems were my stiff white collar and my big brown overall. Willy saw me struggling with both. 'You didn't 'ave to wear that collar and tie, son – perhaps your Mum can turn the sleeves and bottom up for you,' adding with a laugh, 'This job'll put a few inches on you, just you wait and see.'

As the country moved out of the Depression years, new housing estates were springing up all around, at Loughton, Epping, Woodford, Romford, Gidea Park and beyond, and we were delivering to them all.

'How's your new man doing, Willy?'
'He's fine, guv, willing and very capable, no problems at all.'

On the following Friday there was an extra 2s 6d in my wage packet. I told Willy. 'Pop in and see the guv,' he advised me. I thanked my new mate Willy Jenkins too! And Mum and Dad were pleased for me.

Once, loaded up with a delivery to

Billericay in Essex, Willy said, ''Ere comes old Bert Higgins. He's been to Southend on a moving job, you can bet.'

Seated high up with his mate and holding the reins of two lovely big cart horses, Bert's pantechnicon drew up beside us.

'Had a good trip, Bert?'

'Been out of his way, down at Ilford for two days,' Bert replied with a laugh.

'See you in the 'Avelock' later – on me,' Willy said, adding, 'Old Bert loves his 'orses.'

'Don't he drive?' I asked.

'Bert, drive? Wouldn't be seen dead behind the wheel of this!'

'I'd love to learn.'

'I'll teach you if you like, son.'

'Honest?' I asked.

'Course, why not?' was his reply.

The new arterial road to Southend-on-Sea had opened recently, starting at the end of Eastern Avenue, where the first roundabout in the district was built, and threading its way past Billericay,

'''Ere comes old Bert Higgins. He's been to Southend on a moving job…'''

Wickford, Rayleigh and eventually Southend. 'More customers for Harrison Gibson's,' big Willy used to say – and how right he was. 'Ribbon development' followed, with new estates, mostly semi-detached houses each with a garage, built by look-ahead developers with their eyes on the future.

Making a return journey back to Ilford in the late evening on a summer's day, I asked, 'Why are we stopping Willy?' He got out of the cab and walked to my side. 'Move over, son, and let's see what you can do behind the wheel, eh?'

Of course the arterial road in those

Leslie – never when we have a load on, mind – so keep it under yer 'at, all right?'

'Trust me, Willy. Trust me.'

Off we went, and after a few weeks Willy said that I was 'a natural'. I was thrilled. Three months after that first go, I could drive with confidence any of Harrison Gibson's vans. I had so much to thank big Willy for.

Mum and Dad decided that the house in Chadwell Heath wasn't big enough for all of us, so we moved to a larger house in Barking.

On most Sundays I and my two pals

"'...let's see what you can do behind the wheel, eh?'"

days saw little traffic, especially so in the late evenings. I had watched him for some months now, and I'm sure he sensed this. 'This is between ourselves,

would spend the day out on our bikes. Waiting to turn out of our street into Ripple Road, I spotted two girls doing likewise on the opposite side of the road.

'Crikey,' I thought, 'She's a "smasher".' I had no eyes for the other one, only the lovely looking fair-haired girl.

'Come on, Leslie, get a move on,' my pals urged me. I looked back, but disappointed as they had gone the other way!

This happened on a few Sundays. 'Blow it!' I said to myself. 'I'll make up an excuse that I can't make it next Sunday.'

'Got a date?' they both asked. If only they knew!

Miracles do sometimes happen, because that Sunday the girl was on the opposite side of the road, all by herself. A bag of nerves, I waved, and she waved back. 'Where's your friend?' I asked.

'Oh, Jean's gone to Southend for the day with her family.'

'Where you off to then?' I nervously asked.

'Wanstead Park perhaps'.

'Er, er, er, can I come?'

'If you like,' she replied.

'What's your name?'

'Nellie. Nellie Byers. What's yours?'

'Leslie Barker. I like your bike.'

'Do you? Mum and Dad bought it for me for my birthday.'

'When's that?' I asked cheekily.

'The 9th of December,' she replied.

I will never ever forget that Sunday morning. Till then it had been the happiest and most fortunate day of my life!

My dear Nellie and I were married in 1931. At that time I was a driver

'Miracles do sometimes happen, because that Sunday the girl was on the opposite side of the road...'

with my own mate, and earning £2 17s 6d a week. Willy Jenkins came to our wedding; he was now an 'in-house' furniture porter, helping Sid Norman arrange and dress the lavish window displays.

For a time we lived in an upstairs flat in Colombo Road, Ilford. Once a month or so, depending on how many miles were under the bonnet, we drivers would have our vans serviced in the garage by the garage foreman and his two mates, and would spend the day in the nearby warehouse doing odd jobs if there was little else to do. I would help out in the garage, cleaning this and doing that. I loved driving and I was becoming increasingly fascinated with what was happening under the bonnet – so much so that the garage foreman (I forget his name) offered to loan me an instruction manual on how everything did work. Apart from that, Nellie was an avid reader and a member of the Ilford Library, and I often used her card to borrow *The Motorcar Engine and How it Works*.

Monthly magazines were becoming available in bookshops and Nellie would treat me to the occasional one – all about motors, of course! One day, driving back to Ilford after a day's delivery and passing the recently opened Smith's Motorcar Showroom at Goodways, a notice in the window caught my eye. I stopped up the road and said to my mate, 'I shan't be

'...I am looking for a new foreman to run the garage...'

five minutes.' The notice read, 'Unskilled man wanted for weekend work in garage. Apply within.'

The lady at the desk said, 'You want Mr Williams. You'll find him out the back.'

'I'm fixed up for Saturdays,' he said. 'What about Sundays, 8.30am until 5 o'clock? £1 10s, bring your own overalls.'

'Can you make it an extra five bob?' I asked.

'You've a cheek! Oh, all right then – start this Sunday and don't be late.'

I told Nellie later, and she said, 'You and your blooming motor engines.'

'It will be extra money, love,' was my response. 'Will you be all right by yourself on Sundays?'

'Oh, of course I will. Tell you what – I would like to try my hand at decorating, but it's not our place.'

I said, 'Yes, but I want it to look nice.' I was secretly pleased.

Under the guidance of one of Smith's mechanics I learned so much, and dear Nellie turned out to be a dab hand at decorating. I boasted to her, 'When we get our own car I'll be able to do all the repairs, love.'

About 1936 or thereabouts the Dispatch Foreman informed me, 'The General Manager wants to see you, Leslie.'

'Me? What for?'

'I don't know – but smarten yourself up. His office is on the ground floor.'

I did as he

suggested, and tapped on the door, wondering what it was all about. Crikey, perhaps he's had a complaint or something!

'Come in. Ah, Barker, you have been with the company five years or so, right?'

'Er, that's right, Sir.'

He went on. 'Alf the garage foreman is retiring in six months. People speak well of you, and I've heard that you spend your Sundays down at Smith's at Goodways.'

This was a bolt out of the blue. 'Who, me, Sir?'

'That's right. Smith's manager is a great friend of mine. I made him aware that I am looking for a new foreman to run the garage, and he suggested you.'

'Me? But...'

'No buts about it – we're looking for a young man to replace Alf, with lots of energy and get up and go – understood? Mr John, our Chairman, is seemingly not too happy about the general state of our vehicles. He saw one up at Chigwell, the driver with his head under the bonnet. "Should be delivering furniture, that's

his job, not tinkering about under the bonnet," he told me. The vans require more elbow grease on the paintwork, too,' he went on. 'Can you handle it? Think about it for a week and come back and see me. That's all.'

'Thank you, Sir,' I said as I hastily made my way out of his office.

'Nellie, Nellie!' I leaped up the stairs of our flat in Colombo Road, and she hurried out of the living room.

'Whatever is the matter, Leslie?'

'I've a chance of another job – garage foreman.
What do you think about that?'

'It means that you can finish at Goodmayes,' she said. 'No more Sunday work,' she added.

'Don't know about that – I've to see what the job entails.'

I was to find out when I took it on! The manager spelled out the details: 'With the position, Barker, goes a small amount of chauffeuring for Mr John and his family – I will have you fitted out with the necessary uniform, etc, which you will be expected to wear on such

*'The vans require more elbow
grease on the paintwork, too...'*

occasions. Of course there will be an increase in wages, in keeping with your extra responsibilities, understood?'

I understood all right – the extra money was paramount. I was 28 or thereabouts and we were hoping to raise a family.

When I made sure that the vans were spotless on leaving the yard, there was the usual tittle-tattle: 'Don't know who he thinks he is these days...'

I would put them right. 'I'm your new foreman, understood?' They soon came round to my way of thinking and became as proud as I was to see the name Harrison Gibson's on sparkling clean delivery vans.

The first chauffeuring job I had was to bring young Mr Jack, as he was known, back from Haileybury in Hertfordshire, at the end of term. I gave the Buick limousine an extra polish and struggled into my uniform, complete with peaked cap. Nellie ought to see me now, I thought.

It was the end of the summer term, a hot sticky day with a stiff breeze. I was late as I sped through the North Essex lanes, winding the windows down – in an instant the wind took my cap off. What an idiot I felt as I chased it across a recently cut wheat field.

Approaching Haileybury I jammed it back on my head, and drove carefully into the quadrangle, which was packed with lads off for their summer holidays. 'Look at this, chaps,' they said as they gathered around the American Buick. 'It's just like you see in those big Yankee pictures. What can she do?' they asked me as I struggled to open the door, but my guess was as good as theirs. Looking all 'know-all'-like, I said, 'About a hundred.'

'Honestly? Gee whiz!' they said, admiringly.

I found young Mr Jack and opened

'What an idiot I felt as I chased it across a recently cut wheat field.'

the back door. 'Not for me,' he said. 'I'll sit up front with you,' then, as we went through the gates, 'Oh, take that silly cap off.' He did it for me and chucked it on the back seat. But as we approached 'Haylands' at Chigwell, and knowing the rules, he reached into the back seat and handed back my cap.

Much to our joy our first child was born in 1933, and was christened John Phillip Barker. Our landlady, in the nicest possible way, asked us to move on, not relishing the thought of her nights being disturbed by our John. New houses were being built at Newbury Park, Ilford. 'How about it, Nellie? I'm doing all right.'

'But will it last, Leslie?'

'I'll make it last – I've got to.'

So we purchased a brand new house, with a garage alongside. The deposit should have been £30, but I persuaded the manager of the Suburban Development Co to accept £20. They were happy days!

Harrison Gibson's opened their furniture store in High Street, Bromley, Kent, a very affluent area on the extreme outskirts of south London. It was purpose-built and 'dressed out' in the Harrison Gibson style, and was to become as successful as Ilford.

The garage became busier as HG's van fleet increased. My chauffeuring duties found me outside Harrods, where Mrs Gibson would occasionally shop, and numerous other West End establishments.

Bringing 'young Mr Jack' back from 'Haileybury' for the last time – he was now 18 – I asked, 'What have you been up to this term?'

'Oh, I've helped to produce a few school plays, and designed and helped to build and paint the scenery, too. I would like to go to RADA,' he added, a bit wistfully I thought. 'But I do believe father has other ideas for me.' So it seemed, for he was soon off to the Furniture Technical College in Hackney, and later to the Reinman School of Design Display and Art. Perhaps it was his prompting that led Mr John to set about constructing 30 'model rooms' on the top floor, all expertly decorated in various fashions, elegant mahogany and walnut, Tudor oak and modern 1930s style. It was a revolutionary display

'"Look at this, chaps," they said as they gathered around the American Buick.'

and an instant success, attracting more people into HG's than ever before, to admire if not to buy. It was a great credit to the Chairman.

Mr John had been in the Worcestershire Regiment in the Great War and had returned home having lost a leg, a great handicap it would seem, but to his employees it never appeared to be! Mr Jack proved to be a very able right-hand man for the Chairman, but his love for theatre, films and entertainment never diminished.

'Mr Barker, that huge loft over the laundry and what have you that we have up at "Haylands" – I've got ideas for it.'

'Oh crikey,' I thought, 'what's coming now?'

'I would like to turn it into a small cinema, seating about two dozen, just for family and friends of course. With your engineering and electrical experience I am sure we could make a go of it.'

To this day I don't know how, but it all came about – a silver screen, not huge of course, but big enough, two projectors, adequate seating, curtains to draw across the screen. 'I would have liked them to be electrically operated. How about it? I'm sure you can fix it.'

'Whatever,' I thought.

A friend of mine at GB Electronics at Goodmayes saved the day. 'Leslie, find yourself an old bike and strip it all down, leaving the wheels, pedals and chain. Bolt it to the floor, upside down, of course, and I'll find you a little motor.'

'I don't want to pay for it.'

'Leave it to me – between us we'll sort it out.'

'Mr Pottle,' I asked the Soft Furnishings Buyer, 'have you got a remnant of wine-coloured velvet?'

'What for?'

'Mr Jack.' Magic words indeed. They were made, and curtain track installed. With bits of wire and odds and ends borrowed and scrounged, we held our breath as my GB pal pressed a button. 'Hey presto' – like any cinema, the plush velvet curtains moved silently and smoothly across the screen. It was the icing on the cake! I wired in the projectors, installed a dimmer, and wired in extra electric lights. The upholstery shop had renovated some rows of former cinema seats that Mr Jack had come across, and he recruited half a dozen young ladies from a local cinema, complete with uniforms, who were willing to be usherettes on one Sunday evening every month. The big night came. Mr Jack had a last look around, tried the curtains for the umpteenth time, and checked the Jessie Matthews film. Having two projectors meant that while one was projecting the second was loaded and waiting to take over when the first expired. I operated the second. 'Brilliant, Mr Barker, absolutely brilliant!' The showman in John Gibson Jnr shone brightly that night. It was a huge success, and the takings at the box office – about £30 – went to a local charity.

I got myself a motorbike and sidecar, and when time permitted we visited our parents, proudly showing off our little John Phillip. However, the happy days came under threat as war clouds gathered. In September 1939 the lights were turned off in HG's windows in line with other shops and stores as the blackout was enforced – we were not to see them switched on again until the early 1950s. With others I received my call-up papers, never expecting to be turned down as unfit for military service – a throw-back to my childhood days of lengthy illnesses. Nobody, it seemed, needed my services. I felt a bit rejected, but was given the grand title of 'Petroleum Officer' of Ilford and District, meaning that I controlled, on precise instructions from the Ministry of Fuel and Power, the number of petrol ration coupons I was to issue to each company in my area, and had to account for every one issued.

In 1939 John Gibson Jnr joined the Artists' Rifle Brigade, was mobilised the day war was declared, and was commissioned in 1939, joining the 24th Battalion of the Essex Reserves in the spring of 1940. With other furniture stores of those days, we sold utility furniture – devoid of any of the styling of pre-war days – as furniture manufacturers turned their workforces over to more important war work.

'Barker – arrange for two of your vans to go to Bournemouth.' The Chairman handed me the address, saying, 'They're to pick up some furniture for me!' They

'...he recruited half a dozen young ladies from a local cinema, complete with uniforms...'

came back loaded to the tail boards with superb, finely carved oak furniture that had obviously been in use for many years. Fortunately we still retained many of our cabinet-making and polishing staff, extremely skilled men, who were too old for military service. They soon restored these second-hand pieces to their former pristine condition, and they were put on sale. Our Chairman, despite the war years, once again kept Harrison Gibson's far ahead of its rivals, who only had utility furniture to offer in their windows!

Now promoted to Major, John Gibson, his show-business instincts still alive, soon realised that among his battalion were natural-born comedians, singers and actors, so he formed a successful revue party, who gave their first performance, 'Out of the Rag Bag', at Chester le Street, Co Durham. Like all things he took on, it was a success. When training and time permitted, the company was invited to do eight shows around the country for the troops and civvies alike, the last one at the Commodore Cinema at Ryde on the Isle of Wight. The company was dispersed in 1943-44 when the battalions of the Essex Regiment became involved in preparations for the invasion of Europe.

Major Gibson was involved with his battalion in the desperate attempt to relieve the paratroopers who were trapped at Arnhem, immortalised in the film *A Bridge Too Far*.

At long last the war was finally going the Allies' way. Yankee uniforms were as commonplace in the UK now as British ones, and victory in the bitter Battle of the North Atlantic was within our grasp. The Allies had landed in Italy, and there were more bombers in the skies over Northern Europe than we had ever experienced in the dark days of the early 1940s.

'…the last one at the Commodore Cinema at Ryde on the Isle of Wight.'

Then 6 June 1944 heralded the historic announcement that the Allies had made successful landings on the Normandy beaches.

Not to be outdone, later that year Hitler launched his 'secret weapon', the V-1 flying-bombs, or 'buzz bombs' as we called them. Happily, the Harrison Gibson buildings remained untouched thanks to the vigilant fire-watchers up on our roofs.

Our luck ran out in early 1945, when a V-2 landed on the Super Cinema opposite Ilford Station. The huge blast sent the roof of our polishing shop at the rear of the dispatch department flying. Myself and half a dozen others scrambled up and wrenched the remains of the asbestos roof off, leaving the rafters exposed. A few of the lads hurried around to 'Dicky Bird', the builders in Hainault Street, returning with tarpaulin sheets. I was lucky – my trouser turn-ups caught in a long rusty nail protruding from a rafter, and I was hanging head down, swinging to and fro like the pendulum of my father's grandfather clock. The old hands in the polishing shop came to my rescue, and thankfully, except for a rush of blood to my head, no harm was done!

There was still a long way to go to Berlin. Victory in Burma and Japan still had to be achieved, so there was heartache still for so many families who were to lose their loved ones right to the bitter end. That came in May 1945, and, soon after, in the Far East in August, when the first atomic bombs fell on a war-weary world. My parents were to pass away during the following years.

Our second son, Graham Barker, came along in 1947, and as our two boys grew, we wanted more space, which Nellie and I found at Levitt Gardens, Seven Kings. Shortly before Graham was born, the Chairman sent for me. Mr Jack, back from the war and now Managing Director, sat alongside him.

'Ah, Barker, sit down. We wish for you to manage the Dispatch Department,' adding, 'Find a good garage foreman to take over from you.' Mr Jack chimed in, 'Of course I will wish to interview him.'

'Will do, Sir, and thank you.'

Smith's Motors at Goodways helped me out again. 'Yes, I have an excellent man here, he'll jump at the chance of working for HG's. I don't want to lose him but would not wish to stand in his way.' So Jock Mason became our new garage foreman to look after the ever-increasing number of vehicles.

The Chairman got himself a permanent chauffeur and a Daimler limousine, while 'JG' drove himself about in a pre-war Austin saloon. An old-established furniture store, Wells of Bedford, was acquired and was soon to have the HG's presentation style imposed upon it.

At 9.05am I could expect a visit from the Managing Director; it was his first port of call.

'Morning, Barker.'

'Morning, Sir.' Thankfully the vans had departed for the day's deliveries.

'I've been thinking, Barker.' (Oh dear, I thought to myself…) He went on. 'The Display Department wants more space, so too does Mr Cook our ticket writer. With the promotion ideas I have in mind they'll certainly require the space to put them into being. I want them to take over the ground floor of the Mart – yes, all of it.'

'But Sir, what about the furniture stored there awaiting delivery instructions?'

'Mr Barker, you've two other floors in the Mart.'

'Yes Sir, but it's occupied mostly by Mr Gingell's recent buys.'

'In that case he wants to get them across the road on display and around the branches. Look, just see to it, will you?' and off he went to the polishing and cabinet shops, upholstery and curtain sewing rooms and every other nook and cranny in the store.

Jack Davies called in – he was foreman of the cabinet shop. ''Ere, Mr Barker, Mr Jack wants me to get him a fully equipped tool chest – glue pots, screws, everything bar the kitchen sink. He's given me a long list of one-by-threes – 12-foot lengths. I shall want an order from you to get this lot,' adding, 'It's to be in the Mart for Sunday week!'

I reached for my order book, wondering what this was all about! I was soon to find out.

'Mr Barker, have the display people leave the place tidy before they go off on Saturday and arrange for Murray [our caretaker who lived above the Mart] to lay on tea at, say, 11am and 4pm for about a dozen people. The Wanstead Players have asked me to produce their first play of the season and they are coming in on Sunday to build the scenery, under my supervision of course.' Who were the Wanstead Players, I wondered.

The existing stage in the Grove Hall,

Wanstead, where the Players performed, was enlarged, a proscenium was erected, and stage lighting was hired from Strand Electric, which, with Jock Mason's help and know-how, I installed. Furniture was hired from the Old Times Furniture Company of Chiswick. Robinson's the theatrical costumiers dressed the players for *The King Maker*, and a professional make-up artist was engaged. Some months later the curtain went

'...I was hanging head down, swinging to and fro like the pendulum of my father's grandfather clock.'

be the leading Amateur Theatre Company in the land.' Playwright Terence Rattigan said, 'The Players' production of my *Adventure Story* equalled if not bettered the West End production.'

Despite all this activity, HG's nevertheless remained first and foremost a furniture company, and a further company in Ipswich was acquired. In

'...the audience was transported from the Hanging Gardens of Babylon to Alexander's tent at the end of the world...'

up on John Gibson's first production for the Wanstead Players – the first of so many. *The Stage*, the professionals' weekly paper, wrote in later years: 'The Wanstead Players' productions would grace any West End stage – and must

The Author Looked In—And Stayed Three Hours

Terence Rattigan, author of numerous recent West End successes, attended a rehearsal of the Wanstead Players' production of his play "Adventure Story." last week. and stayed for about three hours

He afterwards told the producer, Mr. J. G. Gibson, that he was tremendously impressed with this production of his play by the Wanstead Players, whose standard of acting was the highest he had ever encountered in an amateur company.

Mr. Rattigan will attend one of the performances (April 10th to 15th), probably on the Thursday.

1952 a grand show was put on at Ilford to celebrate 50 years of trading there. The windows were dressed with room settings, displaying Edwardian, 1920s, 1930s, austere 1940s and so-called contemporary early-1950s furniture, each room showing figures dressed in authentic clothes of the life and times of the company since 1902. Other similar shows followed, proving to be hard but rewarding work – but our Mr Jack proved that he could charm birds off the trees in that direction! It seemed that we were all caught up in his boundless energy and enthusiasm. For myself, I now drove a new Morris 8, one of the first off the post-war production line at Cowley, Oxford.

Harrison Gibson's

'Terence Rattigan said, "The Players' production of my Adventure Story *equalled if not bettered the West End production."'*

Sketch design for the set
'the Hanging Gardens of Babylonian
Terence Rattigan
'Adventure Story'.

1953 WHAT THE PAPERS SAID:

'The Players would grace any West End stage.' So said Terence Rattigan, renowned playwright of *Flarepath*, *French without Tears*, *The Browning Version*, and now *Adventure Story*, based on the life of Alexander the Great.

The variety of the scenery designed and painted specially for the players was breathtaking – in a few seconds the audience was transported from the Hanging Gardens of Babylon to Alexander's tent at the end of the world amid the snow and ice of Northern India in BC 323.

1902-1952
Harrison Gibson

The founder
John Harrison Gibson

continued to expand, now to the North of England – Doncaster, Leeds, Halifax, Manchester and Blackburn. Shop fittings got under way – new fronts and interiors were the order of the day! Ilford didn't escape, and while the façade remained the same after the disastrous fire of the early 1920s, much was going on behind. A bridge was built across Havelock Street, connecting the High Road building with the new three-storey premises that were erected opposite. Additional display and design staff were employed to cope with the extra work involved. Unintentionally I became involved in every aspect of this – if John Gibson Jnr should ever write his memoirs, perhaps I'll discover why! After all, I was still the Dispatch Foreman, but deep down I knew I enjoyed it all and wouldn't have wished it any other way!

JG had left the family home, 'Haylands' at Chigwell, and moved up west to Stirling Street, Knightsbridge. The builders moved in and, with the company's decorators and with the usual race against time, endeavoured to complete the job. Before departing on his monthly trips to the north, he would always say, 'Pop into Stirling Street, Barker, and gee 'em all up.'

Jim Carr, the foreman, said in desperation, 'Mr B, look I've stripped off ten layers of wallpaper on the staircase – any more and the place will collapse.'

'Oh, all right, Jim, get the lining paper on and get going with the wallpaper.' I've never seen a speedier paper-hanger than our Jim Carr – excellent work he did, too. The light

fittings went up, the kitchen was installed and the carpets laid, and Harry Elias cleaned all the windows. The lads were loading their bits and pieces into the van and I was vacuuming the carpet when JG's taxi arrived from Euston. He came in and walked slowly round. I could see he was as pleased as Punch, and so were we when he said, 'Let's all have a drink at the pub on the corner.'

Next morning as usual, just after 9am, he came into my office at the back of the dispatch department. 'I was very pleased with all the effort at Stirling Street – it's looking grand. I shall want a housekeeper of course, a general factotum, butler-cum-cook-cum... Oh, I'll leave it to you.'

Me and Harry Robbins, the furniture buyer, accompanied him on a tour of the warehouses. 'I just don't know Robbins, doesn't anybody make anything besides this so-called "contemporary" stuff? Oh, I know all about G Plan and Meredew and the like being our best-selling lines.'

'We still do well with the more traditional pieces,' replied Harry.

'Yes, I realise that, but look at it all – it reminds me of coffins propped up on legs.'

A bedroom of the 1930s, displayed with others from the Victorian, Edwardian, 1920s, 1930s and contemporary eras in an exhibition to celebrate 50 years of trading.

the well-known English names were also still on display – Wedgwood, Royal Doulton, and Royal Worcester. On the hills above Nice and Marseilles in the South of France small studios were found, specialising in other extremes of design – at sensible prices, too. The

'House beautiful', built in the store to display the Italian furniture.

Harry glanced at me and raised his eyebrows.

A fortnight later a concerned Harry came into the office. 'He wants me to go out to Italy with him. He believes he can find what he's looking for out there.'

He did, too! A month later, superb copies of Louis XIV and baroque furniture turned up at Ilford – tables, chairs, chests, exquisite occasional pieces, antiqued and gilded as only Italian craftsmen knew how – the likes of which, the real thing of course, could only be seen in Sloane Street and thereabouts, costing a small fortune. But now we could offer our customers copies of the real thing at a fraction of the price! Of course, it was an attraction for our more affluent customers, but it nevertheless sat happily with the contemporary furniture of the 1950s. It was a success. The china buyer accompanied JG on his next trip, coming back with pieces from the studios of Capodimonte, Fornasseti and many others, glittering light fittings, chandeliers, and wall sconces in elaborate shapes and sizes. Of course,

china gift departments in the Harrison Gibson group took on the appearance of Aladdin's caves!

In March 1959, when JG was in Italy with Harry Robbins again, disaster struck. Out of the blue our Ilford store, which over recent years had been added to, modernised, and effort expended by one and all, and on which thousands of pounds had been spent, was totally destroyed by fire. The phone rang in my home at Levitt Gardens. 'Terrible news, Mr Barker…' the voice said – to this day I do not know who it was. When I arrived, the whole building had collapsed into the basement and the fire was creeping across the bridge into the new building opposite. It had engulfed the small shops alongside, and Moulton's departmental store was ablaze. I couldn't believe my eyes. How could this happen in such a short space of time? Hours later, and now surrounded by many of the staff – a few of the young girls from the china department had tears in their eyes – we watched as the fire was finally overcome, leaving the old Mart where old Bertie Higgins's horses used to be stabled, untouched.

'Come on,' I said to them all, 'there's no point in standing about here – nothing we can do. Take tomorrow off. Come and see me in the Mart the day after tomorrow.' I walked slowly back up Havelock Street accompanied by, I imagine, the local fire chief. He informed me that brigades from all over Essex and the London area had been on site. I looked across the huge black hole where the remains of what had been described as the finest furniture store in the UK and Europe lay smouldering. I was aware that the traffic, held up for hours, was moving along the High Road again.

I couldn't help but think of that day in 1931 when I had donned that brown overall and Willy had said I could take the white collar off and get my Mum to turn up my overalls because they were a bit on the long side.

Oh – I forgot to mention that I had been appointed General Manager some years before. Good Lord, how the time had flown by. I glanced at my watch – crikey, it was getting on for 12. At the top of Havelock Street a familiar figure appeared. I recognised JG with Harry Robbins alongside. 'You

didn't waste much time, Sir.'

'No, we were lucky – got the first flight out of Milan when Mr John phoned me with the news.'

'Lucky?' I thought.

'Well, it's a b— mess, Mr Barker. We'll have to start all over again.' Harry nodded his head in agreement. He took one last look and the waiting taxi took him off to

'"Terrible news, Mr Barker..." the voice said...'

'Haylands'. He lowered the window. 'See you in the Mart in the morning.'

I took Harry Robbins round to the garage in Ley Street, where our cars were parked. I got into my company Triumph and went off home to Nellie, who ran a bath for me, saying, 'You could do with a cup of tea. I'll bring one in.' Dear Nellie, I thought, what would I do without you? She sat on the edge of the bath. 'Is it as bad as I've seen on the television?' I nodded. 'I'm sorry, Leslie, I really am.' She had sorted out my old gardening trousers, shoes and scarf, and as I left she handed me my old cap.

'I don't want this.'

'Put it on,' she insisted. 'They say it's going to be cold today.'

We soon got the Mart organised. The old roof was hidden by draped muslin, coconut matting or something similar was laid over the floor, and dozens of willing hands painted the walls. I was housed in a vacant office in the estate agent's opposite in Hainault Street, answering countless telephone calls from anxious customers. Harry Robbins ordered furniture from suppliers who were anxious to oblige HG's. Clifford's of Vauxhall, who were a few days earlier working in the proposed new restaurant above the recently opened showrooms, knocked out the windows in the Mart,

long-ago boarded up, and fitted the new ones. Percy Cook, our ticket writer, high up on a scaffold painted 'Harrison Gibson temporary showrooms'. Believe it or not, we were open for business four days later, boasting a furniture display, a small china shop and a soft furnishings department, with some table lamps all wired in and lit up. It was almost like the showroom across the road. The Chairman and Managing Director made their way slowly around, congratulating one and all on our achievements of the past few days.

JG's involvement with the Wanstead Players was now over – there was too much to be done in other directions. Thousands of pounds had been raised for local charities during his time with them – I wonder if they still exist today! I often think of those days when I was roped in as chief electrician, scene-shifter and goodness knows what else.

Within a few weeks outline architectural plans were drawn up, and John Gibson urged the Planning Department to give them their approval – let's face it, Ilford Borough Council was as anxious as he was to fill the enormous gap in the High Road. More designers were taken on in the design department, for at this time the Bromley store was being enlarged, also including a restaurant, I believe. During those anxious days our Managing Director never for one moment neglected the other stores and was as vigilant as ever in ensuring that they remained in front of our rivals. We managers had our own 'bush telegraph' – I would phone Doncaster and inform the manager that JG had left King's Cross on the 8.30am and would arrive at 10.20am, and my colleague would make a quick inspection of the windows and showrooms, and greet the Managing Director at the front door. He did likewise when JG departed for Leeds, or wherever. Somehow I sensed the Managing Director knew what was going on.

Back at Ilford final plans were approved, and artist's impressions and models were made. Managers of each department were asked for their opinions, alterations were made, and made again, and new equipment was sent to handle the varied merchandise. Carpets were displayed on frames that could be raised and lowered, and thousands of carpet patterns were suspended in cabinets that customers could view with ease. Illuminated cabinets displayed objets d'art from around the world, and each furniture manufacturer was allocated their own space. G Plan, Meredew, Nathan, Old Charm – all the 'big guns' and the pick of the smaller ones were to be shown in room and other settings. Every effort was made to display all the exciting merchandise of the day to its best advantage, not forgetting the superb Italian pieces and light fittings that graced our store before the fire.

The new store slowly – quickly, I should say – came up out of the ground. Adjoining shops that had been destroyed in the fire had been purchased, making the frontage bigger than before. As each floor was vacated by Gilbert Ash, the builders, our design/display teams, together with our own shopfitters and Messrs Clifford's, the leading shopfitters of those times, moved in. Christmas 1959 came and went, and June 1960 was chosen as the opening date. Of course, for all concerned it became a desperate race against time. David Hicks, the well-known London interior designer, was allocated his space to advise customers on furnishings and decorations

Our own design team, led by Ken Kimberly, were, after weeks of planning, beginning to show what they were made of. By Easter the carpet, soft furnishings, china and lighting departments were

HARRISON GIBSONS

D.BRISTOW

staff over the years, gently coaxed by you-know-who, the giant chandelier in all its magnificence was finally hung in the reception area and glittered and gleamed above the artificial trees and rock pools.

At 4am on that June morning, the 16th, I helped the Managing Director roll out the purple carpet in the reception area, with its two reception desks on each side of the front doors, and placed the comfortable seating on it. I looked up at the clock over the two lifts - it was 5am, 'Let's have one last look around, Mr B,' said JG.

'Back at Ilford final plans were approved, and artist's impressions and models were made.'

more or less structurally finished, each floor boasting approximately 23,000 square feet. But we had another four floors to go, not forgetting the huge window displays to be completed! As the days grew shorter the working hours for all grew longer. But with that 'never say die' attitude ingrained in all HG's

'Our own design team, led by Ken Kimberley, were, after weeks of planning, beginning to show what they were made of.'

Each floor was now strangely quiet, except for the display people putting their final touches to this and that. Reg Pottle, the soft furnishings manager, was filling up the last shelf with his precious pieces of fabric.

'Morning, Sir! Morning, Mr B!'

Then up to the china and lighting departments, where Mr Thomas, with his army of assistants, was dusting his displays for the umpteenth time.

Up to the furniture floors, where old Harry Robbins, the furniture buyer with his assistant, was checking that every piece had its price label on it.

'Well, Mr B, I think we've done it. How long ago was it?'

'Fourteen months, Sir – not bad at all.'

'I'm off to "Haylands" to tell the Chairman how things are.'

I accompanied him to the Bentley outside, then went off to Seven Kings, echoing JG's thoughts – not bad at all. We had just completed half the store – Gilbert Ash were still behind the scenes completing the second part – and with two large restaurants on the very top, where one would be able to view St Paul's to the west and the Thames Estuary to the east. Let's face it, the job was only half finished! But I put my feet up for an hour and was back at Ilford just after lunchtime.

A large pale blue bunting curtain, draped festoon-fashion from the first floor to the pavement, concealed the elaborate window displays, having been put in place overnight with permission of the local authorities. An enclosure of sorts had been erected on the opposite side of the High Road for the VIPs, and closed-circuit television cameras were installed on each floor to enable the hoped-for crowds to see what was going on.

At precisely 6.45pm, eight trumpeters of the Royal Artillery Regiment in ceremonial dress took up their positions on top of the canopy that projected out over the Arcade. The VIPs were shepherded to their enclosure, people were gathering, and the police deemed it necessary to close the High Road to traffic as the crowds swelled to beyond everybody's expectations. More colour was added as Grenadier Guardsmen came marching down the High Road to take part in the proceedings. At 7 o'clock on the dot, to a fanfare of trumpets, the festooned curtain slowly rose to reveal the elaborate window displays and the interior beyond. High up on the roof, 350 pigeons were released by members of the Ilford racing pigeon club, followed by 10,000 balloons.

Led by the Chairman and Managing Director, the VIPs, local dignitaries, TV personalities and manufacturers made their way up the arcade and were ushered into the waiting lifts that took them up to the large reception area on the fifth floor, where they were seated in front of a rostrum from which the Managing Director gave a short speech welcoming them to the new Harrison Gibson store. He gave thanks to all those who had been involved, pressed a button and slowly a bronze bust of a young Ilford couple emerged from beneath the platform, to whom he dedicated the store. The Reverend Ratcliffe Lewis then gave his blessing to the store and all who worked in it!

The Managers and staff guided the VIPs about the store. Meanwhile, in the High Road below, young and old in their hundreds gazed into the windows and watched on the closed-circuit cameras what was happening on the various floors above. The local paper wrote that it was like a Royal occasion – nothing had been seen like it before in Ilford. 'A building years ahead of its time,' it said. 'Furniture displays that must rank with the finest in Europe and the USA.'

It was a memorable evening, and the store opened for business at 9am the next morning. Plans were made for the second part, including the two restaurants!

Meanwhile Nellie and myself were concerned by Graham's health. He had asthma. His teacher at school was concerned that he could well fail his eleven-plus due to the many days he had been absent. How wrong they were! He followed in John's footsteps and attended Ilford County High School and was offered a university place in the North of England. Taking his GP's advice, we moved from low-lying Seven Kings to higher ground in Chigwell, and moved to a bungalow in Tomswood Hill. Graham's health improved, but he had no desire to take up his place at the university. John was meanwhile realising an early ambition; he was at Guy's Hospital, where, after five and a half years of intensive study and a year in the wards, he joined a practice in Woodford as a General Practitioner.

To our surprise Graham followed the same path, and as I write he is a consultant anaesthetist in one of the largest hospitals in East Anglia. After serving some years as a GP, John was invited to take up the coroner's position in Walthamstow. He accepted and was to become the youngest coroner ever to hold the position in London. Nellie and I had indeed two sons to be proud of.

Credit squeezes and the stop-go policies of the Government in power at the time didn't help High Street trading in the early 1960s. Nevertheless Harrison Gibson's was committed to completing the second part of their new premises – we lacked a bedding department, kitchen department and others that were deemed necessary for a complete furnishing store such as ours. The work therefore went ahead with the same speed as that of the first phase.

The 'Room at the Top' restaurant, with its express lift from the pavement, was decorated in traditional style, with elegant blue damask fabric wall coverings. French-style furniture was tailor-made in Italy, and a white Sicilian marble dance floor was laid, complete with a raised rostrum on which cabaret acts could perform. Spotlights were concealed in the elaborate plaster cornices, and on dark dreary winter evenings the London skyline could be concealed by handsome antique gold velvet curtains. Glittering chandeliers hung above the finest tableware, and French and Italian waiters were employed. An elegant bar completed the scene. On the terrace outside, high above the rooftops of Ilford, a superbly fitted kitchen served both the 'Room at the Top' and the adjoining 'Chariot Wheel' restaurant, less expensive but just as expensively fitted out, in true Pompeian style, with its magnificent tile mural some 12 feet high by 100 feet long, specially executed in the South of France. It had a Greek-key-pattern suspended ceiling, with concealed lighting threading its way above tiled table tops and the Pompeian décor below. It was a complete contrast to the traditional room next door, and catered for the daytime shopper. Both were opened in July 1961, and the remaining floors in the store were finally finished.

A glittering array of cabaret stars entertained in the 'Room at the Top', such names as Dickie Henderson, Adam Faith, Diane Dors, Petula Clark, the Beverley Sisters, Jimmy Edwards, Ron Moody and Bob Monkhouse – I could go on! I was invited to the grand

to receive superb copies of 'Early American Colonial Furniture', Italian and French provincial, together with lavish copies of Spanish-style furniture with elaborate wrought-iron work and deeply enriched carvings, all with superbly comfortable upholstery to complement them, in fabrics that we hadn't seen the likes of before. I must say it opened all of our eyes, in particular those of the British furniture industry. The only people who complained were our porters and delivery staff, who had to manhandle it – it was as solid as it looked, and was extremely heavy. Along with it all came the necessary trimmings, table lamps, pictures, objets d'art, and so much else to

opening night. Later the Chairman and his wife celebrated their Gold Wedding Anniversary in the 'Room at the Top' – a night to be remembered.

In 1964 or 1965 our Managing Director was off on his travels again to America. Prior to this he had moved from one side of the Brompton Road to the other, to a fashionable four-storey Edwardian house. Today it would be described as having been given a 'make-over', but I would put it more strongly than that! It was described in the *House and Garden* magazine of the day as being 'one of the most imaginatively designed and elegant homes in Knightsbridge'. In America JG travelled from the north down to Carolina and Mexico in the south, and returned excited with his new furniture and furnishing finds. Existing furniture displays were removed from one whole floor, and our display design team got to work to create new settings that frankly surpassed their recent achievements. Room settings were built

complete the room settings.

Furnishings International on our 6th floor was officially opened by Mrs Bruce, wife of the American Ambassador to London. JG had pulled it off again! A similar show was opened at Bromley the following year – like all HG's events it brought in the crowds, including celebrities of stage, TV and the sporting world. I remember serving a then unknown Mr Bernie Eccleston.

Mr John Gibson Snr, our Chairman, died in 1966. It was a sad occasion. The cortège came along the High Road and halted for a few minutes outside the store that he had so lovingly built up.

'Nellie?'

'Yes Leslie.'

'When I retire, which is soon now, would you fancy a bungalow by the seaside?' 'Honestly, Leslie, do you really mean it?'

'Of course, why not?' I replied.

'Where?' she asked. 'It can't be too far away from the boys, can it?'

I thought about Frinton – Frinton-on-Sea. 'We can go up there this weekend and have a look round.'

After weekends of searching, we found our bungalow by the seaside, and my retirement day in 1968 was a happy, and sad, occasion for me. I said my goodbyes, to Dolly on reception, Nellie at the switchboard, Arthur Platt, Dennis 'the Menace' Cassey, so-named because he had a reputation of landing all the big-spenders that came into the store, Harry Elias, Jack Davis, Jim Holliday and Bert Dawe in the cabinet and polishing shops, and so may others who had served the company so well over the years.

That's it, I thought, as I drove home to Tomswood Hill. Oh no it isn't, thought the powers that be above – you've another 25 years inside you, Leslie, just you wait and see. My lazy days by the seaside were not to materialise just yet awhile. If I am fortunate enough and time permits, I'll be pleased to tell you of them!

POSTSCRIPT:
I remain in touch with 'Young Mr Jack' – he is now 82!

The games we played

STREET CRICKET

Howzat! Up would go the cry as the bowler would be convinced that he had caught the batsman leg before wicket. Back streets of Britain of course were not the car laden, busy and often dangerous places they are today!

A Dustbin for a wicket, a bat if possible or a suitable piece of wood if not, plus a ball and a few mates, and a game was on! These were innovative times and we made do with what we had to hand...

Old Mad Mop

We queued up at Delamura's ice-cream cart for a ha'penny ice wafer and hurried back to sit on the railings outside Mr Dixon's corner shop. It was too hot for any street games! Albie Gibbs came running round the corner – Albie always ran, never walked.

''Ere, Old Mad Mop's up at the top!'

Hot or not, we couldn't afford to miss the fun up at the top, so we went chasing after Albie. Grandad was sitting on a stool on our doorstep at number 83 and was enjoying his *Daily Herald* in the late afternoon sunshine. I've never seen Grandad move so quickly. 'Where are you off to, lad?' he called to me.

'Up the top!' I called back. 'To see Old Mad Mop.'

He grabbed hold of my braces. 'Oh no you're not, my lad. Get inside the house.' I'd never seen my Grandad look so angry.

'We're only looking for a bit of fun,' I endeavoured to explain.

'Find your fun in the back yard, boy.'

I took the small tin bath off the top of the mangle and filled it with water, from the tap in the scullery, and floated

my model boats in it, dejectedly pushing them about with my finger. Ten minutes later Grandad came out with his stool and sat down beside me.

'Look, Kenny, I didn't mean to shout at you, but you're old enough now for me to explain to you about "Old Mad Mop" as you and your mates call him. You've heard us talk about my son, your Uncle George, who never came back from France in the Great War. My lad was in the Rifle Brigade and so too was

your "Mad Mop". "Mad Mop" suffered
terrible injuries and was shell-shocked.
It may have been better if the poor chap
had never come back, like my George.
Come back or not, they were all bloody
heroes boy, and don't you ever forget it!

'So, tell your mates as I'm telling you,
and perhaps they'll stop tormenting the
life out of the poor chap! Promise me
you'll do as I ask.'

I looked down at my model ships in the
tin bath and gave one a push with my
finger. 'I promise, Grandad, I promise.'

'Good lad, good lad,' he said, and went
back to the front doorstep with his *Daily
Herald*, waiting for Mum to come home
from work.

Later that evening, after supper, I
crept into the parlour. The picture was
lovely, all surrounded with embroidered
silk flowers, in a big frame. At the top,
embroidered like the flowers, it said, 'He

gave his life for King and
Country'.
I looked down,
saying to myself, 'I never
knew you and "Mad
Mop" were heroes, Uncle
George.'

*'...Grandad came out with his
stool and sat down beside me.'*

More games we played

Hop-scotch

Believed to date back at least as far as the Roman Conquest of Britain – having been played by Roman foot-soldiers – this was, and for some still is, a popular street game. Often played with a stone or the ever-adaptable bean-bag, the game is played on a series of squares marked out on the playing surface – playgrounds and pavements being the most popular – in 1-2-1-2 formation. Each square is then numbered from 1 to 14 (or more!). Play starts by throwing the stone into a square, then hopping from square to square in numerical order until the square in which the stone lies is reached. The stone is picked up and the player endeavours to hop back to the start. This process must be achieved without the foot crossing a line!

The paving slabs used in Britain's streets provided the ideal 'natural' playing surface. How times have changed, with many paving slabs disappearing and the use of chalk even seen as unwanted graffiti!

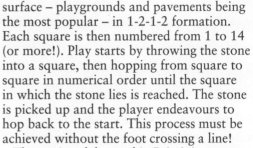

Skipping

Skipping has been played for centuries, usually by little girls. There were many, many skipping songs that were chanted to the beat of jumping the rope. To skip with someone else, a minimum of two people were required; in this instance one end of the rope was tied to the school railings. However, some playground skipping games could involve up to 10 or 20 people, individuals being eliminated if they touched or stopped the rope. These games would involve jumping in and out of the rope while chanting the skipping song. One such songs was 'Dr Banardo's a very nice man, He tries to teach you all he can; Reading, writing, arithmetic, He never tries to give you the stick; If he did you would dance out of England into France, out of France into Spain, over the hills and home again.' Participants would jump in and out at various points of the chant until the end was reached, when the next girl would jump in to continue the game.

Still popular today, skipping is played in school playgrounds up and down the country.

The Speedway Days

Remembered by Alf Barrett

We waited for the traffic lights to turn red and crossed the Barking Road up at the top, then turned into Prince Regent's Lane. Like the hundreds of other supporters, I was sporting my claret and blue scarf that Mum had knitted for me.

'No good queuing for a trolleybus,' Dad said. 'We may as well walk.'

It was Tuesday night, Speedway night, and it was a great night out for us East Enders in the 1930s!

We hurried down Prince Regent's Lane with the others that had now swelled into thousands. I glanced across to our local school football pitches before we crossed the Becton Road – it wouldn't be too long before the footer season started. Thinking that, I would have to ask Dad if he could afford to buy me a new pair of football boots!

Football was forgotten as we made our way down Freemasons Road to Custom House, the home of the 'Hammers' Speedway Stadium. We joined Chas Mount and his Mum and Dad in our favourite spot, and a great roar went up as the 'Hammers' team was announced, followed by the Wimbledon team. The announcer's words were lost as Tiger Stevenson and Bluey Wilkinson made their first appearance of the night. They said in E13 that it was useless going up to bed before 10pm on Tuesdays – what with the roar of the powerful machines and the 30,000 or so crowd, sleep was impossible until long after the meeting was over and the crowd had dispersed.

It was an important meeting tonight – the league championship depended on the result. Tiger and Bluey won their heat, so did Eric 'Ricky' Chitty and Tommy Coombes. An hour later, with the 'Hammers' well in front on points, the roar went up as if West Ham FC had won the Cup Final, as it seemed certain now that the 'Hammers' were champs of the speedway league. Wimbledon, New Cross, Hackney Wick, Belle Vue, Harringay and the rest were nowhere in sight.

A happy crowd eventually made their way back down Prince Regent's Lane.

''Ere, Chas,' I said as we made our way home, 'can't we make our own speedway track down Gongola Road?' adding, 'We could chalk it out with bends by the lamp-post outside Albie Gibbs's house. The starting line could be outside Dixon's corner shop.'

'Oh yeah? And what do we do for bikes?'

I replied, all excited now by my idea, 'We've got our own push bikes and so have our mates, or what about skates?'

The idea slowly took hold of Chas. 'Cor, Alf, it'd make a change from cricket, and we won't break any more windows, will we? I prefer our bikes meself.'

... Mr Ledman came out to collect the horse manure

On Wednesday night after school we chalked out our imaginary track, the bend, as we agreed, being outside Albie's and the starting line stretching across the road outside Dixon's. Of course the usual arguments followed: who would be Tiger Stevenson and who would be Bluey Wilkinson? As usual we tossed up for it; long-legs Charlie was Tiger Stevenson, I was Eric 'Ricky' Chitty, Billy King became Bluey Wilkinson, and Tommy Coombes's lot fell to Eddie.

Podgy Comber didn't have a bike, his Dad saying that he wanted it for getting to work, so Podge became starter, umpire and the rest of it! He held the tape taut, one end tied to old Ebbage's front railings, squeezed the trigger of his water pistol – Charlie got soaked – then let go of his end of the tape and we were off!

Chas reached the bend first, his outstretched long right leg, just like Tiger Stevenson's, saw him safely round the bend, and crouching low over his handlebars, the granite chips flew up off the road, just like the cinders down at the stadium track! He raced on for the bend outside Albie's, I was next, and Eddie was close behind, then his front wheel touched my back one, and off our bikes we came. I picked myself up with two grazed knees, but Eddies looked at his front wheel, which had hit the kerbstone. 'Cor, look at it! It's all buckled up!'

Albie Gibbs sat on the railings outside his house laughing his head off! Of course our long legs came in first and claimed the three points; he was the fastest thing on two wheels down the street – four wheels, too, on his pram-wheeled go-kart.

We turned Ed's bike upside down, Chas fiddled about with the wing nuts

'We turned Ed's bike upside down, Chas fiddled about with the wing nuts and, hey presto, the front wheel ran true again.'

Personal recollection...

Now my business instincts came to the fore: I would collect horse dung and flog it to keen gardeners at a penny or twopence a bucket, negotiable according to quality. As business increased I made a barrow (pram-wheel type), the idea being to amass one shilling so my brother and I could buy two sixpenny all-day tram tickets, and by that means we explored London, all the bridges, the docks area, up the Monument, and on to the South Kensington Science Museum, the Imperial War Museum – not all in one day, of course. The trips depended on the viability of the 'Dung Business', but all the museums were free entry, and St Paul's – an endless list.

N. E. Wheeler

and, hey presto, the front wheel ran true again. Chas wasn't fond of footer, or cricket come to that, but with nuts and bolts and things like that he was a wizard in our eyes! Also, being the only

Boy Scout among the lot of us, he was there when it mattered! And nobody could make a tent on Wanstead Flats like Charlie Mount.

Cricket and footer were forgotten in those dying days of summer, as speedway became the latest street craze, and it wasn't long before all the local streets around us had their local teams, having pinched the idea from us – but we were the only 'Hammers', the rest being the also-rans in our eyes, the Belle Vues, New Crosses, Harringays and the rest of them. Of course, our Tiger 'Long Legs' Stevenson beat the lot of them. Between heats old Mr Ledman came out to collect the horse manure that had fouled up the track. Fearing for his safety, we took his shovel and bucket from him and filled it for him. 'Cor, thanks, boys – this'll do just nicely for me roses!' Autumn came and with it the dark nights, and the latest craze was put aside for football. I got my new boots.

Sadly, after the war speedway lost its appeal and in the 1950s the league was disbanded. A vast new housing estate covers the site where the famous old stadium stood – with no roars for Tiger and Bluey on their bikes, they must all get a good night's sleep! Me, Ernie and Ken, two old school pals from Balaam Street School, often meet up and take a stroll around our old Plaistow haunts. Dongola Road's parked cars are nose to tail from one end to the other – our make-believe speedway racing of 65 years ago would be an impossibility these days.

'What a pity that young people of today don't seem to have the fun and excitement that we lads, with our own initiative, enjoyed all those years ago,' I said.

Later, when we called in for a drink and a bite to eat at the old Black Lion, Ernie, looking thoughtful, said, 'You know, if I told my grandchildren of all the supposed fun we had in our young days I'm sure they would say, "Oh Grandad, you were still living in the Stone Age! Look what we have today: TVs, videos, computer games, our own mobiles. We don't even have to go out to find our fun."'

Ernie's comment put a damper on what had been, until then, another enjoyable meet-up with the two old school pals.

When I arrived home, a bit late, Beryl, my wife, said, 'Goodness, I thought it was us women that had all the chat!'

'I know love, we do go on a bit.'

POSTSCRIPT:
Chas Mount emigrated to Australia in the mid-1960s and joined an engineering company that had its headquarters in the UK. Thirty or so years later he retired as Chairman, a 'nuts and bolts' man all his working life. He now resides on Queensland's Sunshine Coast, and we still keep in touch.

West Ham Speedway
"The Hammers"
Recalled by Alf Barrett

Speedway was introduced into this country in the late 1920s and was popularly known as 'dirt track racing'. The first meeting was claimed to be held at High Beach, near Epping. One of the pioneers was an Australian promoter, Johnny Hoskins, who went on to promote the West Ham speedway team up to the out break of the Second World War.

The 'Hammers', as they were known, competed at the local Custom House stadium, which matched the size of Wembley Stadium but not the glamour. The team of the 1930s was captained by 'Tiger' Stevenson, but probably the most popular, and certainly the most spectacular, rider was 'Bluey' Wilkinson. 'Bluey' won the World Speedway Championship at Wembley Stadium while nursing a broken collar-bone that was strapped for the finals. English and Australian riders dominated during those early years and the popularity of the sport was best illustrated by the 'FULL HOUSE' attendance at the World Championship, held annually at Wembley Stadium.

Other riders from that era included:

Jack and Norman Parker (brothers)
Eric Langton
Bill Kitchen
Tommy Coombes
Ron Johnson
George Merton
Lionel Van Praag
Jack and Geordy Milne (American brothers)
Arthur Arkinson

During the English season, which traditionally started on Good Friday evening (at the Custom House track) and lasted through to September, five England versus Australia test matches were held, again attracting full attendance.

The national league consisted of seven teams, each holding its meetings on its own special evenings, ie Wimbledon on Monday, West Ham on Tuesday and New Cross on Wednesday, etc.

The teams were Wimbledon, West Ham, New Cross, Wembley, Harringay, Belle Vue and Hackney Wick (later replaced by Bradford).

The biggest track, at 440 yards, and also the fastest, was the Custom House circuit, the home of West Ham.

Not so fond memories of Fairburn House

Billy Wilkins

It was 4 o'clock and I was leaving the classroom with the rest of my schoolmates when Mr Spinks, our teacher, called, 'Wilkins! I want a word with you. The headmaster wants to see you, so go up to his study.'

Climbing the flight of stairs to his study I wondered what old Nooe wanted with me! I hesitantly knocked on the door.

'Come in! Ah, Wilkins,' he said, as I stood in front of his desk. 'I hear that you're a good footballer, and that at 11 you're playing for the senior team.'

'Er, yes, Sir.'

'Well, I'm recommending you to join Fairburn House Boys' Club, so go along this evening. Take your PT kit with you and ask for Mr Stock – tell him I sent you along. Off you go then.'

I hurried off home to tell my Mum, as it wasn't everybody who had the chance to join Fairburn House! It was a famous boys' club, known throughout East London. Len Goulden, who once played for Holborn Road School, was now a West Ham star and an England international. Jacky Wood, who had played for Fairburn House, was an amateur international, too.

I hurried along Barking Road, went in and asked a group of lads where I could find Mr Stock. 'That's him over there.'

I introduced myself to Mr Stock and explained, 'My headmaster has sent me along to see you, Sir.'

'All right, lad. Get changed and join the other boys – we're having PT tonight.'

I joined them, helped get the vaulting horse into the middle of the hall, and laid the large coconut mat behind it.

'Get in line then!' Mr Stock called out as he took up his position alongside the horse. I took my place at the end of the line. 'Nothing in this!' I thought, as I waited my turn; I had done it so often at school. I ran up and vaulted over with ease. What happened next I don't remember. Instead of landing on my feet, I fell on my outstretched left arm!

'You all right, lad?' an anxious Mr Stock asked.

'It's me arm! It don't 'arf hurt!'

'Stay still, boy, don't move.'

Half an hour later I was in St Mary's Hospital down Upper Road. I heard someone say to my Mum and Dad, 'It's a compound fracture, which means wiring the bits and pieces together. Don't worry, he'll be right as rain in a few weeks!'

My induction into Fairburn House had lasted just an hour!

'About time young Billy Wilkins had a bath. See to it, nurse,' I heard the Ward Sister say. The nurse took me into the bathroom and took the sling off my arm.

'Oh Billy, what 'ave you been up to?' she asked as she looked at my arm, which, by now, had turned as green as the grass on Prince Regent's Lane footer pitches! 'Sit there and don't move,' she told me, and hurried off. I sat there and wondered what all the fuss was about.

She came back with the Sister, 'Old Bossy Boots' we called her. 'Get Doctor so-and-so down here,' she said to the nurse. 'I don't care what he's doing, just get him down to the ward!'

When I woke up I could vaguely see Mum and Dad talking to the doctor.

'Trouble is,' I heard him say, 'your lad's young body has rejected our wiring-up of his fracture. If the worst comes to the worst, we may have to take it off.' The drowsiness came back over me and I fell back to sleep again!

However, my good fortune prevailed and I was up and about again a month or so later, skylarking about in the ward with the other boys – not when 'Old Bossy Boots' was about, of course! Visiting hours in those long-ago days were just one hour each evening, and not always convenient for Mum or Dad. By chance one day in the lav I noticed a small window above the WC. Curiosity got the better of me and I climbed up and opened it to look out. I had a view of the northern outfall sewer bank that passed along the back of the hospital. I told Mum. 'Billy, if you go in there at 2 o'clock every day I'll walk along the sewer bank and wave to you.'

My dear Mum did that for five months, just after she'd been round to Aunt Harriet's to give my cousins, Ken and Bobby, their dinners while Aunt Harriet was out at work.

At long last the day came when I went home, and back to school.

'Instead of landing on my feet, I fell on my outstretched left arm!'

'When can I play football?' I asked my teacher.

'You'll have to get your parents' written permission before we can consider it, lad,' he said. My Dad wouldn't sign the necessary papers, but after I'd got round Mum he did, and I was soon playing for the senior team again, but I never again ventured through the doors of Fairburn House!

'I noticed a small window above the WC. Curiosity got the better of me and I climbed up and opened it to look out.'

POSTSCRIPT:

Bet and I were married in 1947, never realising that we had both been in St Mary's Hospital at the same time! She was in there because her Dad was whitewashing the kitchen ceiling, and when she looked in to see what he was up to, she got two eyefuls of whitewash! Of course, in those days us toffee-nosed 'Plaistowites' never talked to those roughs from Custom House!

How lucky I was, years later during the war, when I was in the Navy, to meet Bet again. It was the luckiest day of my life; we married and were blessed with a son and a daughter, Billy and Rosyn.

What more could I ever have wished for, as I put my memories of those distant days on paper. It is my 78th birthday today, and my dear Bet died on this very day eight years ago.

Bill and Bet on their wedding day

The artist and the admirers

Liz Gwyther

I was born in the middle of Epping Forest – well, not actually in the forest, but in a large Victorian house called 'Suntrap' at High Beech. 'Suntrap' was a large family home and in Victorian times, at the turn of the 1900s, was used as an Isolation Hospital.

During the Second World War the house was used as a maternity hospital for East Enders. I came along in March 1945, the first child of Ken and Edith Gwyther, and was christened Joan. My twin sisters Dinky and Jackie followed some five years later – Dad was upset, as he longed for a boy!

Jackie now resides in Sydney, Australia, while Dinky cares for the elderly in Woodford, Essex. In the early days we three girls shared a bedroom in the attic of our terraced house in West Ham, and

'I shepherded my two younger sisters out through the small window set into the roof, …'

every so often during the winter nights the chimney caught fire; the chimney breast protruded into our attic bedroom, and as the burning soot roared up the chimney, it made a noise like an express train. I had recurring nightmares, dreaming that our house was on fire and that I shepherded my two younger sisters out through the small window set into the roof, followed them up on to the ridge and huddled together, looking down to the terrifying drop to the street below us!

I was an avid reader, and borrowed countless books from the local library. I soon became aware of Joan of Arc's fate, and it haunted me, so much so that by deed poll my name was changed to Elizabeth. I was

'I went feet-feet first into the coal-cellar....'

lavatory. I remember them as being happy days – surprising ones, too, when, being chased out of the scullery by Dinky and Jackie, I went feet-feet first into the coal-cellar. Dear Mum had removed the cover to black-lead it!

My earliest schooldays were spent at Napier Road Infants School. My teacher – I can't remember her name – took Mum aside, saying 'Mrs Gwyther, you will have an artist in your family, cos all she wants to do is to paint and paint and paint.' Later I was fortunate to win a scholarship to Plaistow Grammar School. I quickly

discovered that there was more to my life than longing to paint and draw; nevertheless, the encouragement I received there to pursue my favourite subject led me to

relieved that I was no longer called Joan, and my terrifying memories of fire could be put behind me.

Once a week, summer or winter, the zinc bath was bought into the kitchen, and we three girls took it in turns to bath, then Mum, then Dad – all in the same water! The job of emptying it was a tedious business, first by bucket, then a jug and finally a cup. Dad's brother and his wife lived with us, all sharing one

being granted a pass, when I was 11, by the PLA (Port of London Authority) to take my brushes, pallet and pad to sketch whatever I wanted to in the docks area. My parents couldn't afford the school uniform, but Mum was a wonderful seamstress and made it for me. Dad was a sheet-metal worker and Mum supplemented his weekly wage-packet by playing the piano in our local pubs, Dad

'... to sketch whatever I wanted to in the docks area.'

drinking most of what she earned and more.

At 15 years of age I took my portfolio of artwork to the St Martin's School of Art in Charing Cross Road, and was accepted to do a degree course in Fine Arts. Reluctantly my Mum and Dad said they couldn't afford for me to attend there – I still have the letter of acceptance to this day. Nevertheless, when I left Plaistow Grammar I worked for a millinery company, illustrating their catalogues and advertisements. I was being paid for what I loved doing – I was on my way.

By the early 1970s my friends were 'going up West'. 'Swinging' London with its Kings Road and Carnaby Street and the clubs were the attraction, so not to miss out I followed them and found for myself a tiny flat in Kensington. It was there that I became aware of the Chelsea Arts Club; I joined and became a life-long member. It was there that I met David Parker, a trustee of the club, not realising that the CAC was to change my whole life and take me away from West Ham for ever!

In the late 1970s an artist from the Seychelles visited the club and purchased some paintings of mine, taking them home where he had a friend, the President. They must have impressed the man, because a few weeks later to my astonishment I received an invitation from the President to go to the Seychelles to paint at will. It was there that I was introduced to scuba-diving, never realising before what a wonderful world lay beneath the waves of the Indian Ocean. In the early 1980s I went to the Caribbean to obtain my final qualifications, still painting of course.

My dear Mum in the meantime had moved to Ilford in Essex, where she was diagnosed with Parkinson's disease. I hurried home and helped nurse her for five years. Finally she died there, in 1990. I moved back to central London, and my friendship with David Parker blossomed. He had been a barrister, but his professional life had finally given way to his first love – professional photography. When he retired David purchased a farm in Cumbria close to the Scottish border. I was tiring of the London scene – it no longer held any attraction for me – and David asked me to join him in Cumbria.

Arriving at Inch Farm, the sheer beauty of Cumbria, its ruggedness, its peace and solitude, meant that for me it became the most beautiful place in the world. Cumbria introduced me to a new art form – sculpture. I purchased the necessary tools of the trade and as always couldn't wait to get started! Eventually I was commissioned by Sainsbury's, who had purchased the site for a new store from a well-known local benefactor's heirs on the understanding that a monument would be erected to him, commemorating his generosity to the people of Longtown during his lifetime.

My sculpture now stands on a plinth in front of the new Sainsbury's store in Cockermouth, Cumbria. Soon after this I broke my back in a motor car accident! In hospital I counted my blessings, and thought of the day that Mum and Dad told me they couldn't afford for me to attend the St Martin's School of Art. At that time it made me more determined than ever to realise my ambition of being a self-taught artist, and proud and so pleased to be one. I think Mum and Dad would be too.

Cumbria in Britain's beautiful Lake District
Photo: John Townsend

Remembering the Trolleybus...

was one of the first to abandon this environmentally friendly form of transport in 1921, while Bradford was the last system to close, in 1972. The first London trolleybus, fleet No 4 from Fulwell Garage, ran on 16 May 1931 between Teddington and Twickenham; the conductor was Ronald Hadland.

The last London trolleybus (fleet No 1521) ran on 8 May 1962 between Hampton Court and Fulwell Garage. The driver was Albert West, at the age of 70 Fulwell's oldest driver. On that day Ronald Hadland worked as conductor on the ceremonial run from Twickenham to Kingston on preserved trolleybus No 1.

The trolleybus was once a relatively common site on the streets of many of Britain's towns and cities. The first systems opened on 20 June 1911 in Leeds and Bradford; interestingly, Leeds

TROLLEYBUSES IN BRITAIN

The following is a complete list of towns in Britain where trolleybuses used to run, with their first and last years of operation:

Aberdare	1914 - 1925
Ashton-under-Lyme	1925 - 1966
Belfast	1938 - 1968
Birmingham	1922 - 1951
Bolton	1936 - 1956
Bournemouth	1933 - 1969
Bradford	1911 - 1972
Brighton Corporation	1939 - 1961
Brighton Hove & Dist.	1946 - 1959
Cardiff	1942 - 1969
Chesterfield	1927 - 1938
Cleethorpes	1937 - 1960
Darlington	1926 - 1957
Derby	1932 - 1967
Doncaster	1928 - 1963
Dundee	1912 - 1914
Glasgow	1949 - 1967
Grimsby	1926 - 1960
Halifax	1921 - 1926
Hastings	1928 - 1959
Huddersfield	1933 - 1968
Ipswich	1923 - 1963
Keighley	1913 - 1932
Kingston-upon-Hull	1937 - 1964
Leeds	1911 - 1928
Llanelli	1932 - 1952
London	1931 - 1962
Maidstone	1928 - 1967

Manchester	1938 - 1966
Mexborough/Swinton	1915 - 1961
Newcastle-upon-Tyne	1935 - 1966
Nottingham	1927 - 1966
Nottingham & Derby	1933 - 1953
Oldham	1925 - 1926
Pontypridd	1930 - 1957
Portsmouth & Southsea	
	1934 - 1963
Ramsbottom	1913 - 1931
Reading	1936 - 1968
Rhondda	1914 - 1915
Rotherham	1912 - 1965
St Helens	1927 - 1958
Southend	1925 - 1954

South Lancashire Transport	
	1930 - 1958
South Shields	1936 - 1963
Stockport	1913 - 1920
Teesside Railless	
Traction Board	1919 - 1971
Walsall	1931 - 1970
West Hartlepool	1924 - 1953
Wigan	1925 - 1931
Wolverhampton	1923 - 1967
York	1920 - 1935

*Information kindley supplied
by David R Harvey*

If you enjoyed this book

and would like to receive news of other

nostalgic volumes why not join

Friends of
The NOSTALGIA Collection
www.nostalgiacollection.com / friends

Friends receive regular news of
current, new and forthcoming titles
from *The NOSTALGIA Collection.*

To join simply send a large (A4) SAE to:

The Membership Secretary
Friends of The Nostalgia Collection
The Trundle
Ringstead Road
Great Addington
Kettering
Northants
NN14 4BW

or email:
friends@nostalgiacollection.com